Technology Investigations

Jenny Ridgwell

HEINEMANN
EDUCATIONAL

Heinemann Educational
a division of Heinemann Educational Books Ltd
Halley Court, Jordan Hill, Oxford OX2 8EJ

OXFORD   LONDON   EDINBURGH
MADRID   ATHENS   BOLOGNA   PARIS
MELBOURNE   SYDNEY   AUCKLAND   SINGAPORE   TOKYO
IBADAN   NAIROBI   HARARE   GABORONE
PORTSMOUTH   NH (USA)

First published 1991

British Library Cataloguing in Publication Data
Ridgwell, Jenny
   Technology investigations.
   1. Technology
   I. Title
   607.1

   ISBN 0–435–42006–2

Designed and produced by Gecko Limited, Bicester, Oxon
Printed and bound in Great Britain by Athenæum Ltd, Newcastle upon Tyne

Acknowledgements
The Publishers would like to thank the following for permission to reproduce
copyright material:
Body Shop plc for the product labels and photograph on sheet 58 and the extracts
on sheet 61. British Carrot Growers Association for the logo and recipes on sheet
78; British Electrotechnical Approvals Board for BEAB mark on sheet 33; Campus
2000 for the use of their name on sheet 28; Charity Projects/ Comic Relief
Education Department for the storyboard on sheet 51; Coca-Cola Great Britain for
their logo on sheet 149 ('Coca-Cola' and 'Coke' are registered trademarks which
identify the same product of the Coca-Cola Company);*Colchester Evening
Gazette* for the article 'Botham faces Essex' on sheet 73; Collins/Angus and
Robertson Publishers and Jim Murphy for the illustrations from *Weird and wacky
inventions* on sheet 140; Consumers' Association for the article from *Which*
magazine on sheet 67; Ecole Notre Dame de Cion for the menus on sheet 73; Dr
Dorothy Einon/*Child Education* for the extract 'What makes a good toy' on sheet
133; Emotional Rescue Ltd for the card on sheet 80; *The Guardian* for the article
'Robot Olympics' on sheet 106; Inventalink for the design ideas on sheet 44;
Kelloggs Company of Great Britain Ltd for the package designs on sheet 147;
Kodak Ltd for the logo on sheet 149; Ministry of Agriculture, Fisheries and Food
for the poster on sheet 54, the recipe and circular on sheet 55 and the ration book
on sheet 56; National Magazine Company for the extract from *Cosmopolitan*
'Grasp a carrot' on sheet 76; NERIS for the printout on sheet 84; *New
Scientist*/IPC Magazines Ltd/World Press Network for the article 'Mechanical
athletes totter toward Olympic glory' on sheet 106; Pepsi-Cola International
Northern Europe Division for the logo on sheet 149; Rex International Ltd for the
Bisto cartoon on sheet 146; Gwen Sampson/*Daily Telegraph* for the article
'What's in Santa's sack?' on sheet 103; Science Museum Library for 'A clock that
makes tea' on sheet 27; *The Scotsman* for the article 'How to fend off a killer with
carrots' on sheet 76; Gerald Simmons Wheelchairs for the three extracts and
photograph on sheet 156; Solo Syndication for *The Daily Mail* for the extracts 'Did
you know' on sheet 49, 'Packaging that costs shoppers £6 a week' and 'The Big
Mac boxes clever in cardboard' on sheet 66 and 'Top of the takeaways' on sheet
142; *Toy Trader* magazine for the extract on sheet 133; Toyota Ltd for the logo on
sheet 149; Vico for the packet on sheet 141; Chris Winn for the 'Erf' cartoon on
sheet 53;Trocadero for the logo on sheet 149;

The Publishers have made every effort to trace copyright holders.
However, if any material has been incorrectly acknowledged, we
would be pleased to correct this at the earliest opportunity.

The author would like to thank the following people for their contributions to the
preparation of this book.
Anna-Marie Hlustik (primary teacher)
Ellis Pitt (technology teacher and freelance designer)
Marion Rutland (IT adviser, secondary schools, Wandsworth)

Content

Note: **T** indicates a Trigger sheet, **F** a fact sheet and **A** an Activity sheet

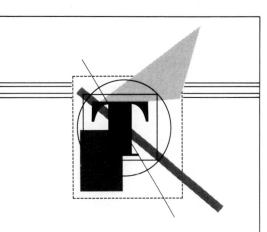

TEACHER'S
NOTES

Covering the National Curriculum

Covering the National Curriculum

Technology Investigations has been written for pupils studying Design and Technology at Key Stage 3 and is designed to help pupils follow the programme of study and meet the attainment targets at levels 3–7. To help teachers plan and record what their pupils have done, the file includes detailed grids showing which statements of attainment and programmes of study have been covered (see pages 10–20). There is also a grid showing how the themes in the file cover the required contexts – **home**, **school**, **recreation**, **community**, **business and industry** – and how they relate to the three outcomes – **artefacts**, **systems and environments** (see page 9). To help with recording there is an assessment sheet which can be freely photocopied and used by pupils and teachers to keep a record of work as it progresses (page 24).

A cross-curricular approach

Technology in the National Curriculum draws in aspects from a range of subjects. The ideas in *Technology Investigations* are therefore cross-curricular with particular attention being paid to Art and Design, Business Studies, CDT, Home Economics and Information Technology. To this end, the file has been written by a team of teachers including CDT, HEc and IT specialists, and a primary teacher.

Information Technology

Information Technology plays an important part in this file and a grid is included to show where such work can be included (see page 24). A list of suitable software for pupils in Years 7–9 is also included in the Resources section (page 23).

Wordprocessing packages can help pupils improve the quality of their written work and their presentation of information. Computer aided design (CAD) programs are valuable for designing on screen. Information can be stored, retrieved and organized using spreadsheets and databases. Other software is useful for questionnaire design and data analysis. Additionally, pupils can make use of data-retrieval facilities such as NERIS, CAMPUS 2000, Teletext and Prestel. *Technology Investigations* provides opportunities for pupils to use these types of program.

The pupil sheets

The bulk of the file comprises photocopiable sheets for pupils. These are divided into four sections to provide ideas and activities for Design and Technology work within the context of a particular theme.

There are three distinct types of sheets for pupils:

Triggersheets These sheets provide pictures to help pupils brainstorm for ideas for discussion and design.

They include historical aspects of design and designs from other cultures as well as up-to-date design ideas.

Factsheets These provide up-to-date back-up information to support the work suggested within the theme.

Activity sheets These sheets can be used for design and make activities or as ideas for further work in class or for homework. Activities are organized under the headings 'Discuss', 'Research', 'Plan', 'Record', 'Design and make', and 'Evaluate'.

All of these sheets can be freely photocopied for use in class or for homework.

The themes

The four themes in the file are:
◆ Introduction
◆ Carrots
◆ Space
◆ Getting around.

These themes have been deliberately chosen to illustrate how one idea can be used in many ways.

Introduction

This theme consists of a series of trigger sheets which introduce pupils to the technical terms needed for work in Technology within the National Curriculum. Pupils (and teachers) need to be familiar with terms such as **mechanism, artefact** etc. and these sheets are designed to stimulate discussion to help this.

This theme also includes three activity sheets to help pupils explore Technology in more detail. 'Trapped on an island' helps pupils to meet their needs when they are isolated and constrained by the materials available on an island. This sheet can also lead to interesting class discussions about the development of technology from early times.

The other two sheets include designs created by others – one fictitious, the other from real designs patented in 1990 – and will be useful for evaluation exercises.

Carrots

The **topics** covered in this theme are:
◆ Bugs Bunny (cartoons and storyboards)
◆ Carrots in wartime Europe (investigating historical sources; preparing recipes; designing a healthy eating campaign)
◆ Carrots for cosmetics (investigating products from the past and present; animal testing; environmental issues of packaging; researching, designing, making, packaging and evaluating a 'natural cosmetic product'; databases)
◆ Herbie – a marketing case study (the redesigning of a school meals system)
◆ Designing patterns using carrots (printing techniques)

- Carrots and your health (investigating carrots as a health food)
- Cooking with carrots (preparing and evaluating recipes)
- Carrot designs (evaluating existing artefacts; designing and making).

The likely **design and technology outcomes** from this theme are:
- Designing and making a storyboard and funny sketch
- Designing and evaluating a healthy eating campaign for wartime
- Researching, designing, making, testing, packaging and evaluating a cosmetic product
- Creating a database
- Investigating past and present school meals systems
- Exploring different printing techniques using carrots
- Preparing a feasibility study on carrots as a health food and acting on it
- Designing a health food using fruit or vegetables
- Preparing and evaluating carrot recipes
- Using carrots to come up with design ideas.

Space

The **topics** covered in this theme are:
- Spacecraft design (exploring the possibilities for spacecraft design, both inside and out; NERIS)
- Space food (investigating variants in diet, including cultural; preparing and evaluating a space meal)
- Space clothes (investigating what is worn inside and outside the spacecraft)
- Choosing fabrics (evaluation and testing of fabrics)
- Computer aided design (fabric designs; designing a name and logo)
- Games (investigating, designing and making games)
- Robots (designing a robot; computer robots; Robot Olympics; laws of control; robots in space)
- Jewellery (designing and making jewellery; investigating jewellery from the past, other cultures and the present; exploring what can be used to make jewellery).

The likely **design and technology outcomes** from this theme are:
- Designing and modelling a spacecraft, both inside and outside
- Designing systems for the spacecraft
- Investigating the possibilities of NERIS
- Investigating the food eaten in space
- Using a computer program to evaluate a space menu
- Planning, cooking and testing a meal designed for space
- Investigating and evaluating the clothes worn both inside and outside the spacecraft
- Designing a uniform to be worn on a space mission
- Evaluating and testing fabrics
- Exploring the possibilities of computer aided design
- Investigating the games played in space, in the past and in other countries

- Carrying out a survey to find which games are the most popular
- Designing a game
- Designing and making a model of a robot
- Exploring floor turtles controlled by the computer language LOGO
- Investigating robotics through the Robot Oympics and laws of control
- Designing and making jewellery
- Investigating jewellery from the past, from other cultures and from the present day
- Exploring what can be used to make jewellery
- Evaluating materials.

Getting around

The **topics** covered in this theme are:
- Safety (safety in the different work areas used in Technology; getting around in safety; role play)
- Toys (toys which go around; safety regulations for toy design; designing and evaluating toys)
- Games (games which go around)
- Bags (designing a bag)
- Moving pictures (zoetrope)
- Whacky ways of getting around (evaluating historical designs)
- Eating on the go (apple crackles; takeaway food; designing a new fast food)
- Product image (name, packaging and logo)
- Wheelchairs (adapting a wheelchair to meet individual needs; designing a wheelchair; investigating wheelchair design specifications; wheelchair sports; evaluating historical wheelchairs).

The likely **design and technology outcomes** from this theme are:
- Greater awareness of safety issues in work areas used for Technology
- Designing a safety system
- Role play of safety issues
- Observing children at play and recording findings in a database
- Exploring toys and investigating their safety
- Designing, making and testing a toy
- Designing a game which goes around
- Designing and making a bag
- Making a zoetrope
- Evaluating historical designs of whacky ways of getting around
- Evaluating a food which can be eaten on the go
- Investigating takeaway food
- Designing a new fast food
- Investigating product images as portrayed through name, packaging and logo
- Evaluating existing logos and coming up with a new design
- Evaluating wheelchair designs and designing adaptations to meet individual needs
- Designing a wheelchair to fit in with a lifestyle
- Exploring wheelchair design specifications and including them in design proposals
- Investigating wheelchair sports
- Historical evaluation of wheelchairs.

Contexts and likely outcomes for pupil activities

Theme	Likely outcomes			Contexts				
	Artefact	System	Environment	Home	School	Recreation	Community	Business/Industry
Carrots								
Bugs Bunny		✔				✔		
Carrots in wartime	✔	✔					✔	✔
Cosmetics	✔	✔						✔
Herbie campaign			✔		✔			✔
Printing with carrots	✔	✔				✔		
Designing a health food	✔							✔
Recipe evaluation	✔							✔
Space								
Space mission			✔	✔				
Space to live			✔	✔				
Food in space	✔	✔		✔				
Clothes	✔			✔				
Games	✔	✔		✔		✔		
Robots	✔	✔				✔	✔	
Jewellery	✔							✔
Getting around								
Safety in technology		✔	✔		✔			
Symbols for safety		✔					✔	
Role play		✔			✔			
Toys	✔					✔		
Games which go around		✔				✔		
Bags	✔							✔
Zoetrope	✔					✔		
Eating on the go	✔	✔						✔
Wheelchairs	✔	✔					✔	✔

Coverage of Attainment Target 1: Identifying needs and opportunities

SoA	Carrots	Space	Getting around
Level 3			
a	49, 51, 53, 55, 56, 59, 60, 62, 63, 67, 68, 72, 73, 77, 78	94, 98, 99, 102, 103, 108, 115, 116	119, 120, 121, 122, 123, 124, 128, 131, 133, 135, 141, 142, 143, 144, 145, 146, 147, 148, 149, 151, 152, 154, 155,
b	49, 53, 56, 59, 60 73	108	119, 128, 131, 152, 155
Level 4			
a		83, 87, 90, 91, 92, 104, 105, 107	125
b	56, 60, 67, 68, 73	90, 102, 103	128, 131, 133, 135, 141, 142, 143, 146, 148, 152, 155
c	56	92	127, 133, 143, 152, 154, 155, 157
d	77	92	
e	59, 67, 68, 77, 78	87, 90, 92, 94, 96, 97, 99, 103	125, 144, 145, 155
f	55, 56, 73	90, 103, 107, 108, 114, 115	128, 131, 140, 146, 147, 152, 158
Level 5			
a	73, 77	103	119, 131, 146, 152
b	55, 56, 59, 60, 66, 67, 73, 77	90, 91, 92, 94, 95, 98, 102, 103, 104, 105, 106, 107, 108, 114, 115, 116	128, 131, 140, 141, 142, 144, 145, 147, 148, 149, 151, 152, 154, 155, 157, 158
Level 6			
a	59, 77	103	128, 142, 144, 145, 158
b		90, 103	
c	60, 73	83, 87, 90, 91, 92, 94, 95, 98, 103, 104, 105, 106, 107	145, 152, 157, 158
Level 7			
a	73, 77	102, 103	
b	59, 73, 77	96, 97, 99, 103	128, 131, 142
c	55, 56, 59, 73, 77	90, 102, 103, 104, 105, 107, 114, 115	128, 131, 143, 144, 145, 149, 152
d	56, 73, 77		133, 135, 146, 152, 154, 155

*Numbers refer to page numbers in this file

Coverage of Attainment
Target 2: Generating a design

SoA	Carrots	Space	Getting around
Level 3			
a	59	83, 87, 90, 92, 99, 105	131, 143, 144, 145, 149, 155
b	49, 55, 56, 59, 60, 62, 68, 72, 73, 80	87, 90, 92, 94, 95, 98, 102, 103, 104, 105, 108, 115	127, 128, 131, 138, 144, 145, 155
c	49, 51, 53, 55, 56, 59, 60, 62, 63, 66, 67, 68, 72, 73, 77, 80	87, 90, 92, 94, 98, 102, 103, 104, 105, 106, 107, 108, 115, 116	121, 122, 123, 124, 125, 127, 128, 131, 133, 135, 138, 139, 140,141, 142, 143, 144, 145, 146,147, 149, 151, 152, 154, 155, 157, 158
d	68	87, 103, 104	135, 154
e	56, 59, 60, 77	90, 92, 99, 103, 104, 105, 108	125, 131, 135, 139, 143, 144, 145, 149, 152
Level 4			
a	53, 56, 59, 60, 63, 68, 72, 73, 77	83, 87, 90, 91, 92, 94, 95, 98, 99, 103, 104, 105, 108, 116	125, 128, 131, 133, 141, 142, 143, 144, 145, 149, 152, 154, 155
b	59, 68	92, 99, 104	
c		83, 104	125, 128
d	59, 60, 68, 77, 80	87, 90, 92, 98, 103, 104, 105	125, 128, 131, 140, 142, 143, 144, 145, 149, 155
Level 5			
a	59, 60	90, 92, 99, 103, 104, 105	125, 128, 131, 135, 139, 143, 144, 145, 149, 155
b		92, 99	144
c	53, 55, 56, 59, 67, 73, 77	90, 99, 102, 103, 108	119, 131, 135, 142, 144, 145
d			128, 138
e	59	90, 103, 105	128, 131, 135
Level 6			
a	59, 60	90, 92, 103	144, 145, 149, 155
b		92	144, 145, 149, 155
c		90, 103	135, 144, 145
d			
Level 7			
a	59, 60	102, 103	
b	60		135, 149, 152
c		102, 103	135, 144, 149

*Numbers refer to page numbers in this file

Coverage of Attainment
Target 3: Planning and making

SoA	Carrots	Space	Getting around
Level 3			
a	49		127, 128
b	51, 55, 59, 60, 68, 77	92, 94, 95, 104, 105, 108	128, 135, 138, 144, 145, 154
c	55, 60, 73, 77, 78	94, 95, 96, 97, 98, 104	120, 135, 138, 139
d			
Level 4			
a			
b	53, 56, 59, 60, 77, 78	103, 104, 108	127, 144, 145, 149, 154
c	51, 55, 60, 78	90, 94, 95, 99, 102, 103, 104, 105	128, 131, 135, 138, 139
d			
e	51, 68	87, 90, 98, 103, 105	125, 128, 149, 154
Level 5			
a			
b		87, 90, 92, 94, 95, 102, 104, 105, 108, 115	128
c	51, 55, 78	87, 96, 97, 102, 104	128
d			
Level 6			
a	49, 51, 55, 60, 68, 78	90, 94, 95, 96, 97, 98, 103	128, 149
b		94, 95, 96, 97, 102, 103, 104	
c		102, 104	
d			
e	56, 77		119, 152
f			119
Level 7			
a		98, 103, 104	
b		96, 97, 98, 103, 104	
c			

*Numbers refer to page numbers in this file

Coverage of Attainment Target 4: Evaluating

SoA	Carrots	Space	Getting around
Level 3			
a	49, 53, 56, 60, 73, 74	92, 104, 105	119, 125, 127, 131, 139, 149, 155
b	51, 60, 73, 74, 78	87, 99, 105	125, 127, 131, 139
Level 4			
a	56, 60	92, 105	125, 127, 135, 139, 144, 145
b	60, 68, 73, 74	92, 99, 105	145
c	56, 60, 63, 66, 67, 68, 80	91, 92, 94, 102, 106, 107, 108, 116	120, 121, 122, 123, 124, 133, 140, 141, 147, 148, 149, 151, 152, 156, 157, 158
d	55, 56, 60, 66, 67	90, 91, 92, 105, 106, 107, 108, 114, 115	135, 140, 141, 142, 143, 144, 147, 148, 149, 152, 155
Level 5			
a	51, 55, 56, 60	87, 90, 105	119, 144, 149, 154
b	73, 74, 78	87, 90, 104, 105	140, 145
c	55, 56	108	119, 135
Level 6			
a		95	
b	55, 56, 60, 77	94, 103, 104, 105	119, 128, 138
c	63, 73, 74, 77, 78	87, 90, 116	156
d	67, 73, 74, 78	87, 105	141
e			
Level 7			
a			125, 127

*Numbers refer to page numbers in this file

Coverage of Attainment Target 5: Information Technology capability (Opportunities for using Information Technology)

SoA	Carrots	Space	Getting around
Level 3			
a	68, 69	87, 97, 98, 99, 102, 104	139, 142
b	49, 53	105	
c	63	90, 97	142
d			
Level 4			
a	60, 68, 69	87, 97, 98, 99, 104	140, 142
b	49, 53	105	
c		90	
d			
e			
f		106	
Level 5			
a	68	87, 98, 99	140
b		105	
c	63	97	142
d		102	
e			
Level 6			
a	68	99	
b		105	
c	64		
d			
e			
Level 7			
a		99	
b			
c			
d		84	131
e			
f			

*Numbers refer to page numbers in this file

Coverage of the Programme of Study for Key Stage 3

Programme of study	Carrots	Space	Getting around
Developing and using artefacts, systems and environments			
Pupils should be taught to:			
◆ analyse the task and its components, to identify those which depend upon the completion of previous tasks, and to develop a flow chart		90	128, 131
◆ set objectives and identify resources and constraints	49, 55, 59, 60, 74	87, 90, 92, 94, 103, 104, 105, 108	119, 125, 128, 131, 135, 136
◆ organize their working to complete the task on time			127, 149
◆ produce a documented plan for their work, including an analysis of the resources required and a time schedule		103, 104	128
◆ select and use mechanisms to bring about changes and control movement		105	128, 138
◆ know that using energy affects comfort and convenience		90	152
◆ use information sources in developing their proposals	55, 56, 60, 77	90, 92, 103	119, 131, 133, 140, 142, 152, 154, 155
◆ analyse a system to determine its effectiveness and suggest improvements	51, 73, 78		119
◆ test simple objects to determine performance.		94, 95, 96, 97	152
In addition pupils working towards level 3 should be taught to:			
◆ recognize pattern in the structure of objects	68		
◆ know that objects are changed by the forces applied to them.		92	
◆ know that systems have inputs, processes and outputs and recognize these in a variety of simple forms	73, 78	83, 98	119
◆ use simple mechanisms to transfer motion		105	128, 138, 140
◆ recognize that a source of energy is required to make things work		105	128, 138, 139, 140, 152
◆ organize their work, taking account of constraints	55, 74	87, 92, 98, 105, 114, 115	119, 125, 128, 131, 135, 136, 143, 144, 145
◆ realize that, when working in teams, people may have specialist roles			149
◆ use a variety of energy devices.		105	128
Pupils working towards level 4 should be taught to:			
◆ make a simple system and consider its effectiveness and whether modifications should be made to the design in order to improve it	51	105	119, 125
◆ test simple objects they have made	60	90, 104	128, 138, 139, 154
◆ recognize that structures have distinctive characteristics including form and stability		86	152
◆ use mechanisms to change one type of motion into another			
◆ recognize that mechanisms need to be controlled if they are to achieve their intended function		105	
◆ take into account the characteristics of different energy sources when designing products			
◆ exercise persistence in their designing and making and recognize when to seek help			
◆ allocate tasks when leading a team.		103, 104	149

*Numbers refer to page numbers in this file

Coverage of the Programme of Study for Key Stage 3

Programme of study	Carrots	Space	Getting around
Developing and using artefacts, systems and environments			
In addition pupils working towards level 5 should be taught to:			
◆ recognize that the control of a system involves inputs, outputs, feedback and stability of that system		104, 105	119, 125
◆ recognize and represent organizational structures	73		
◆ select and use simple mechanisms, including linkages and gearing, in making prototypes			
◆ identify the basic principles of how different mechanisms change speed or change motion, from one form to another			152
◆ recognize that mechanisms can be controlled by computers		105	
◆ understand that it may be necessary to practise an operation in order to improve quality		99	127, 138
◆ take account of the effects of transferring and using energy in their designing and making.		105	139, 140
In addition pupils working towards level 6 should be taught to:			
◆ use methods of releasing and transferring energy in systems			
◆ modify a plan, as necessary, explaining the need for changes	51	104, 105	127, 131, 139, 149
◆ use knowledge and understanding of materials to design and make structures which stand up to stress		105	140
◆ take account of the forces which operate on and influence mechanisms when selecting a mechanism for a design		105	140
◆ recognize aspects of control in a variety of systems, including input, output, feedback and stability			
◆ estimate how long an activity might take, and the resources required and take this into account in their planning,		103	128
In addition pupils working towards level 7 should be taught to:			
◆ know that energy can be a significant cost in manufacture and in the use of a product or system			
◆ recognize that people are an important resource and need to be trained, organized and motivated			119
◆ design and make structures to take stationary and moving loads			140, 152, 154
◆ recognize how the efficiency of a mechanism can be improved when designing a product			
◆ design mechanical systems to produce a desired output from a given input		104, 105	140
◆ estimate the time taken, and the resources required, to complete each task and its components.			

*Numbers refer to page numbers in this file

Coverage of the Programme of Study for Key Stage 3

Programme of study	Carrots	Space	Getting around
Working with materials: **Pupils should be taught to:**			
◆ ensure that the working area is well ordered and safe, and that equipment is well maintained			119, 125
◆ use equipment safely; follow safe working practices and understand the procedures for dealing with accidents		104	120, 121, 122, 123, 124
◆ consider, when selecting and using materials, their physical and aesthetic properties, availability and cost, and the product being made	74	87, 90, 92, 108, 114, 115	128, 135, 136
◆ combine materials to create others with enhanced properties	59, 60, 74, 77	87, 90	
◆ assemble a range of materials		87, 90, 94, 95, 104, 105	136, 138, 154
◆ take account of the constraints imposed by equipment		87	138
◆ working with a variety of media to produce graphic outcomes		98, 99	
◆ apply simple finishes appropriate to the materials used and to achieve a desired effect			135, 136
◆ aim for a high quality of accuracy and presentation	60, 62, 68	87, 90, 98, 99, 104, 108	135, 138, 139
◆ select a match of materials and equipment to create a quality outcome	68	87, 90, 103, 104, 108	128, 135, 138, 139
◆ identify and use machines to perform tasks required by their design activities.		104	135
In addition pupils working towards level 3 should be taught to:			
◆ recognize that materials and equipment need to be safely stored and maintained			119, 120, 121, 122, 123, 124
◆ be aware of the dangers of the misuse of materials and equipment, and the consequent risk of accidents			119, 120, 121, 122, 123, 124, 125
◆ use alternative means of joining materials			135, 136
◆ recognize the appropriate tools for working with a variety of materials.		90, 104, 108	
Pupils working towards level 4 should be taught to:			
◆ recognize that materials have different working properties		90, 104, 108, 114, 115, 136	
◆ recognize the aesthetic qualities of natural and manufactured materials		94, 114, 116	
◆ select and use equipment correctly	68, 74	87, 90, 103, 104	128
◆ check the condition of equipment before use.			
In addition pupils working towards level 5 should be taught to:			
◆ know the working properties of a range of materials		87, 94, 95, 96, 97, 108	128
◆ recognize the purpose of equipment, to understand the way it works, and to use it		104	
◆ identify hazards in the working environment and to take appropriate action if dangerous situations occur.			119, 120, 121, 122, 123, 124, 125
In addition pupils working towards level 6 should be taught to:			
◆ use a variety of material processing equipment to develop craft skills involved in shaping, forming, joining, assembling and rearranging		104, 108	128
◆ select and use appropriate methods of assembling a range of materials		87, 103, 104	128, 135
◆ recognize the purpose of equipment, to understand their handling characteristics, and the basic principles upon which they work.		104	128
In addition pupils working towards level 7 should be taught to:			
◆ use computer-based systems as tools for designing and making	49, 63, 68	87, 90, 97, 98, 99, 102, 103, 104	131, 139, 140
◆ recognize that products must be electrically and mechanically safe.			

*Numbers refer to page numbers in this file

Coverage of the Programme of Study for Key Stage 3

Programme of study	Carrots	Space	Getting around
Developing and communicating ideas **Pupils should be taught to:**			
◆ investigate existing solutions to design and technological problems when developing ideas for new ones	55, 56, 60, 63, 73	86, 90, 92, 102, 103, 108, 116	119, 125, 128, 131, 135, 140, 142, 152, 156, 157
◆ explore a range of potential solutions before selecting one	60	92, 99, 103	127, 128, 131, 138, 143,
◆ know that aesthetic qualities influence consumers' choices	60	108, 114	147
◆ use computer-aided design and draughting techniques	60, 68	87, 98, 99	139
◆ maintain a questioning but open-minded approach when developing their ideas			
◆ take account of human scale and proportion when designing.		83, 86, 87	128, 135, 136, 140, 152
In addition pupils working towards level 3 should be taught to:			
◆ develop a range of simple skills used in drawing and modelling.	80	83, 87, 90, 92, 104	125, 128, 135, 136, 138, 142, 149, 152, 154, 155
Pupils working towards level 4 should be taught to:			
◆ make two- or three-dimensional models of their design ideas and to test these before proceeding further	68		135
◆ extend the range of techniques used in their drawing and modelling	68	87	155
◆ generate ideas and develop them further using a variety of techniques and media.	60, 74, 77	87, 90, 103, 104, 105	119, 125, 128, 135, 136, 143, 144, 145, 152, 154, 155
In addition pupils working towards level 5 should be taught to:			
◆ use specialist vocabulary when communicating proposals		104	141, 143, 144, 155
◆ develop styles of visual communication which take account of what is to be conveyed, the audience and the medium to be used	49, 53, 60, 62, 77		119, 125, 127, 135, 136, 145
◆ present their design and technological ideas and proposals using modelling techniques and specialist vocabulary		104	
◆ recognize the relationship between two-dimensional representation and three-dimensional forms	68	87, 104	135, 136
◆ investigate artefacts, systems and environments to find ideas or new designs.	49, 53, 55, 56, 59, 60 62, 63, 66, 68, 72, 73, 80	86, 91, 92, 103, 106, 107, 108, 114, 115, 116	120, 121, 123, 124, 125, 128, 131, 140, 141, 142, 146, 147, 148, 149, 152, 154, 156, 157
In addition pupils working towards level 6 should be taught to:			
◆ gather, select and organize information for use in designing	55, 56, 59, 60, 73	90, 103, 108	119, 125, 128, 131, 133, 141, 142, 146, 147, 149, 154, 155
◆ know that the generation of many ideas and the development of single insights can each provide the basis for design proposals.		114, 115	119, 143
In addition pupils working towards level 7 should be taught to:			
◆ know how designers and technologists have produced ideas and to make use of similar approaches when designing and making		98, 106, 108, 116	128, 140, 141, 143, 144, 146, 147, 150
◆ collate, sort, analyse, interpret and present information in a form appropriate to the purpose and the intended audience	56, 63, 77	90, 94, 95, 116	119, 125, 139, 143, 144, 145
◆ devise an effective strategy for investigating a specific situation	56, 59, 63, 67, 77	90, 102, 103, 108	119, 128, 131, 133, 142, 143, 144, 145, 146, 147, 152, 155
◆ distinguish between various techniques of modelling and use appropriate techniques for developing proposals.			

*Numbers refer to page numbers in this file

Coverage of the Programme of Study for Key Stage 3

Programme of study	Carrots	Space	Getting around
Developing and communicating ideas **In addition pupils working towards** **level 5 should be taught to:**			
◆ identify markets for goods and services	59, 73	108, 115	125, 141, 143, 144, 154
◆ know that, in the production and distribution of goods, the control of stock is important	73		
◆ plan a simple budget			
◆ investigate the effects of design and technological activity on the environment	63		
◆ establish and apply criteria for assessing: the needs and opportunities identified, the choice of materials and equipment to achieve the design, the procedures adopted, the end result.		104	125
In addition pupils working towards level 6 **should be taught to:**			
◆ integrate drawing, modelling and text in developing a design			
◆ prepare a business plan, including a cash forecast and budget, and monitor performance against it			
◆ know that original designs can be granted patents			
◆ use factual information and value judgements	56, 60, 77	107	131, 133, 140, 152, 156
◆ recognize objective and subjective information	66, 77		
◆ use information and experience gained from appraising products.		92, 108, 116	125, 131, 140, 154, 158
In addition pupils working towards level 7 **should be taught to:**			
◆ understand how market research can be used to measure user needs and market potential	59, 77		142
◆ calculate costs and make decisions on price		104, 115	128, 145
◆ recognize the historical and cultural background to design and technological developments		86, 90, 108, 116	131, 135, 139, 140, 146, 147, 152, 158
◆ recognize the relationship between price, cost, income and competition in the market for goods and services		115	
◆ use different ways of assessing the effectiveness of a solution		90	125
◆ work together to establish criteria for appraisal			

*Numbers refer to page numbers in this file

Coverage of the Programme of Study for Key Stage 3

Programme of study	Carrots	Space	Getting around
Satisfying needs and addressing opportunities **Pupils should be taught to:**			
◆ consider the influence of advertising on consumers	77		142, 145
◆ identify markets for goods and services and recognize local variations in demand		116	
◆ investigate the effects of design and technological activity on the environment, and take account of its impact	59	114	
◆ recognize that the preferences of consumers can change		108	142, 152, 158
◆ recognize that economic, moral, social and environmental factors can influence design and technological activities	55, 56, 59, 63	90, 91, 114, 116	119, 131, 135, 142, 143, 144, 145, 146, 147, 152, 155, 157
◆ recognize potential conflicts between the needs of individuals and of society.			127
In addition pupils working towards level 3 should be taught to:			
◆ know the importance of exploring needs and opportunities before proposing solutions		87	152
◆ recognize that a solution may result in problems in other areas		114, 115	
◆ consider how well their products are designed and made	55, 60, 68, 74, 77, 78	87, 90, 103, 104 105, 108	128, 139
◆ propose simple modifications to improve the effectiveness of designs and to overcome difficulties when making	51	87, 104	125, 139
◆ reflect, individually and in groups, on how they went about their work, and whether changes might be needed.	74	87, 92, 98, 104, 105	125, 131, 145
Pupils working towards level 4 should be taught to:			
◆ propose modifications to improve the performance and appeal of existing products			141, 152, 154, 158
◆ know that advertising helps promote and sell goods and services	77		145
◆ know that costs include time, people, skills, equipment and materials		108, 115	128, 135, 143, 145
◆ make judgements about products designed and made by others	74	92, 106, 116	140, 141, 147, 156, 158
◆ evaluate the outcome of their activity against the original need, and propose modifications that would improve the overall quality of the outcome	56, 60	87, 104, 105	119, 125, 131, 135, 145
◆ reflect on how they went about a task, and how they might plan their next task differently.			125, 127, 145

*Numbers refer to page numbers in this file

Technology resources

General books

Tom Baird, *Communicating Design*, Heinemann Educational
Keith Good, *Starting CDT*, Heinemann Educational
McCafferty, *Research Skills*, Edward Arnold (three volumes)
Gwen Gawith, *Library Alive!: Promoting Reading and Research in the School Library*, A & C Black
M J McNeil, *How Things Began*, Usborne Publishing Ltd
Mills and Stringer, *Oxford Choices*, Oxford University Press
Jenny Ridgwell with Louise Davies, *Skills in Design and Technology*, Heinemann Educational
Jenny Ridgwell, *Skills in Home Economics: Food*, Heinemann Educational
Jenny Ridgwell with Louise Davies, *Skills in Home Economics: Technology*, Heinemann Educational
Jenny Ridgwell with Louise Davies, *Skills in Home Economics: Textiles*, Heinemann Educational
Tristram Shepard, *Education by Design: A Guide to Technology across the Curriculum*, Stanley Thornes
Tristram Shepard, *Introducing Design and Technology across the Curriculum*, Hutchinson
Tristram Shepard (ed), *Ways Forward*, Stanley Thornes
Kay Stables, *Starting Textiles*, Macmillan
Wright and Royal, *Approaching Design and Technology*, John Murray
Design and Technology in Process: Health and Fitness, Heinemann Educational
Managing Design and Technology in the National Curriculum: A Coordinated Approach, Heinemann Educational

Places to visit for design ideas

Design Council, 28 Haymarket, London SW1Y 3DX
Regular displays of work by people of all ages
Design Museum, Butlers Wharf, Shad Thames, London SE1 2YD
Regular turnover of exhibits, facilities for pupils to do workshops, research library available

Booklets and files for general ideas

Art and Craft Design Technology
published by Scholastic
D: Student design, The Big Paper, Designing
all published by the Design Council, 28 Haymarket, London SW1Y 3DX
Design a dessert
published by Tesco
Food for thought – the Sainsbury Gallery: A resource pack for teachers
published by the Science Museum Education Service

Sainsbury's publish a study pack full of information about their organization. They will also provide a free lecture service for pupils.

For further research

Carrots

Books
Joe Adamson, *Bugs Bunny: Fifty years and only one grey hare*, Pyramid Books (1990), Octopus Publishing Group, Michelin House, Old Fulham Road, London SW3 6RB
North Yorkshire Education Catering Services, *Herbie's Herald*, sponsored by Craigmillar, Sussex House, Burgess Hill
Waller and Vaughan-Rees, *Women in Wartime*, Macdonald & Co

Cosmetics
The Body Shop Book, available from Body Shops (£7.95)
Leaflets and further information also available from The Body Shop International plc, Sussex BN17 7LR

Packaging
Finding out about packaging, Hobson's Publishing plc
The Tidy Britain Group, The Pier, Wigan, Lancashire WN3 4EX
The Blue Peter Green Book, BBC Books, Sainsbury's

Dyes and dyeing techniques
Dylon International, Worsley Bridge Road, London SE26

Places to visit
Imperial War Museum, Lambeth Road, London SE1 6HZ
Exciting simulations of bomber missions, displays of wartime Britain and experience in an air raid shelter
Museum of Advertising and Packaging, Gloucester

Space

Books, leaflets and packs
The Young Scientist Book of Spaceflight, The Usborne First Guide to the Universe, Usborne Publishing Co Ltd
Primary Science Pack
Earth and Space Association for Astronomy Education, ASE, College Lane, Hatfield, Herts AL10 9AA

Computer Software
ORRERY – software which simulates a journey through space
Food program – for diet analysis
Drawmouse – for designing patterns and shapes for clothing
Autosketch – for plans and designs of spacecraft

Places to visit
Science Museum, Exhibition Road, London SW7 2DD
Exhibition on Space Gallery, Food for Thought (good teacher support material)
The London Planetarium, Marylebone Road, London NW1 5LR
Useful to trigger ideas for Space

Getting around

Books, leaflets and packs
Ballam, *Safety at work, home and in between*, Edward Arnold
Safety in Practical Studies, DES
European Standard Safety of Toys 1988, British Standard (1989), BSI, Linford Wood, Milton Keynes, MU14 6LE
Kate Greenaway's Book of Games, J M Dent & Sons Ltd, Aldine House, 26 Albemarle Street, London W1X 4QY

Oxford Dictionary of Nursery Rhymes, Oxford University Press (1951)
Kenneth and Marguerite Fawdrey, *Pollock's History of English Dolls and Toys*, Ernest Benn Ltd (1979), 25 New Street Square, London EC4A 3JA
Boots Quality, The Boots Company plc, Merchandise Technical Services, 3 Wilford Road, Nottingham NG2 3AA (tel 0602 866671)
Boots catalogue (available from shops)
Mothercare catalogue (available from shops)

Useful addresses
Age Concern, 1268 London Road, London SW16 4EJ
British Standards Institution, 2 Park Street, London W1A 2BS
Early Learning Centre, South Marston, Swindon, SN3 4TJ
Home and Leisure Accident Research, DTI, 10–18 Victoria Street, London SW1H 0NO
Royal Society for the Prevention of Accidents, Cannon House, The Priory, Queensway, Birmingham B4 6BS (tel 021 233 2461)
Royal National Institute for the Blind, 224 Great Portland Street, London W1N 6AA
Royal National Institute for the Deaf, 105 Gower Street, London WC1R 6AH
Tesco House, PO Box 18, Delamare Road, Cheshunt, Herts BN8 9SL

Places to visit
Museum of the Moving Image, South Bank, Waterloo, London SE1 8XT – stimulating material on zoetropes, cartoons and film making
Bethnal Green Museum of Childhood, Cambridge Heath Road, London E2 9PA

Computer software
Text processing and desk-top publishing
Newspa – a program which can be used to prepare school newspapers
Caxton – offers a wide range of fonts, useful for logos and names

Graphics and painting packages
Art and time – a simple painting package for producing pictures; can be used for animation
PC Paintbrush, PC Paintbrush plus – easy to use painting packages for labels and images
Image – useful for drawing images and plotting squares; can repeat patterns
Mosaic – images are made from coloured squares; can repeat patterns
Drawmouse – useful for patterns; can repeat images; zoom facility
Autosketch, Autocad, Lincad linear graphics – computer-aided design packages which can draw rooms, plans and nets for packets
Spreadsheets
Logistix, Multiplan, Grasshopper (Newman College) – useful for entering data which needs manipulating (adding, subtracting, etc)
Databases
Grass, Excel, Find – can be used to store, sort and retrieve information
Datafiles
Quest, Accidents, Migration plague, Health data (Revolver) – contain useful data on health problems
Subject specific
The Food Program, ILECC (£25.00)
Survey, ILECC (£15.00)

National Curriculum: Technology Record Sheet

Design idea

Name

Outcome

- Artefact ☐
- System ☐
- Environment ☐

Context

- Home ☐
- School ☐
- Community ☐
- Recreation ☐
- Business/Industry ☐

Materials used

Information Technology

		AT1	AT2	AT3	AT4
Level 3	a				
	b				
	c	■			■
	d	■			■
	e	■		■	■
Level 4	a				
	b				
	c				
	d				
	e		■		■
	f		■	■	■
Level 5	a				
	b				
	c	■			
	d	■			■
	e			■	■
Level 6	a				
	b				
	c				
	d	■			
	e	■	■		
	f	■	■		■
Level 7	a				
	b				■
	c				
	d		■	■	■

Heinemann Educational *Technology Investigations*

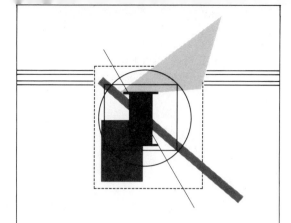

INTRODUCTION

Artefacts

Systems

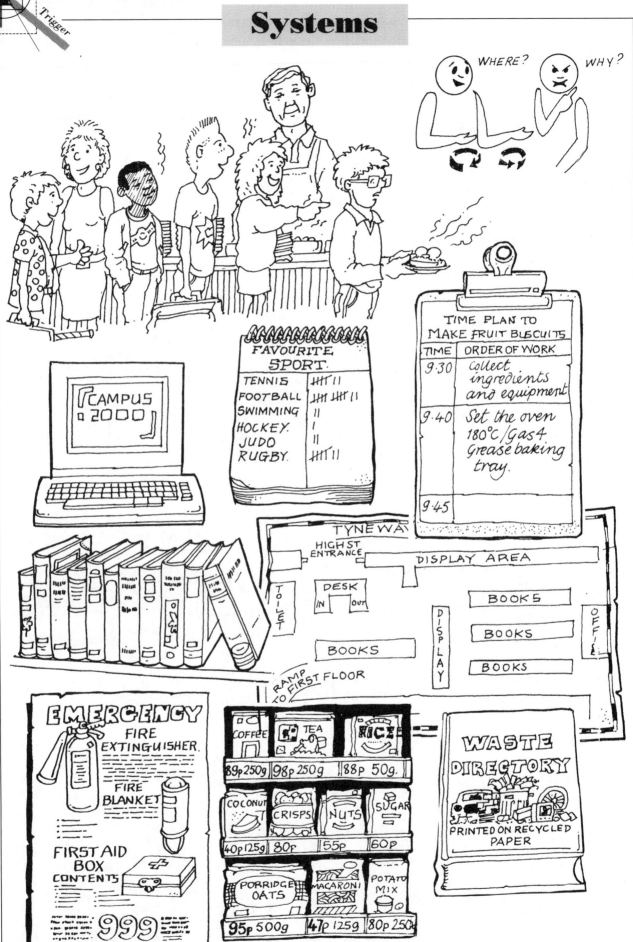

Heinemann Educational *Technology Investigations*

Environments

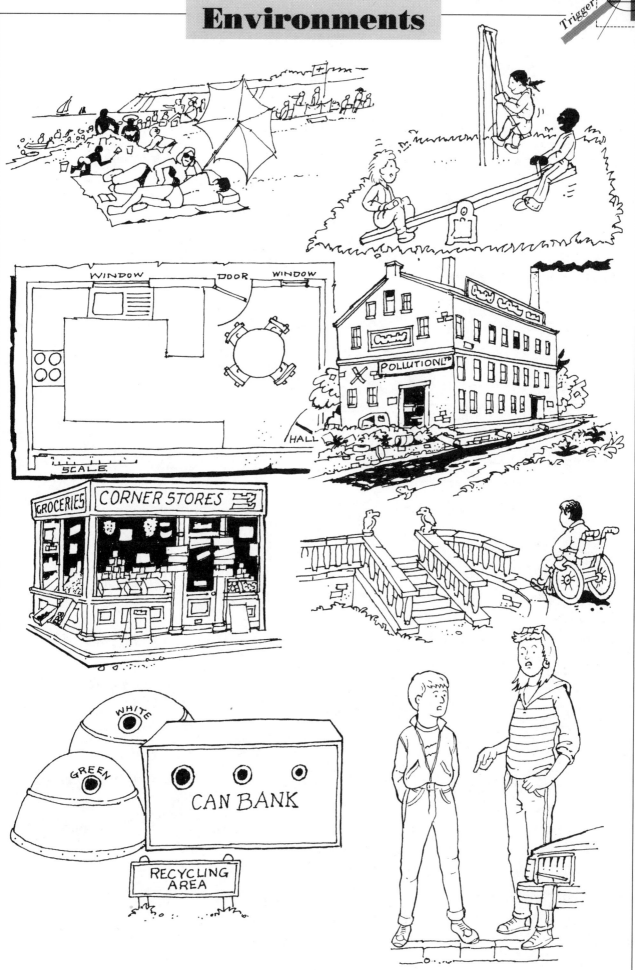

Heinemann Educational *Technology Investigations*

Needs

Heinemann Educational *Technology Investigations*

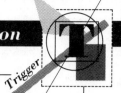
Equipment

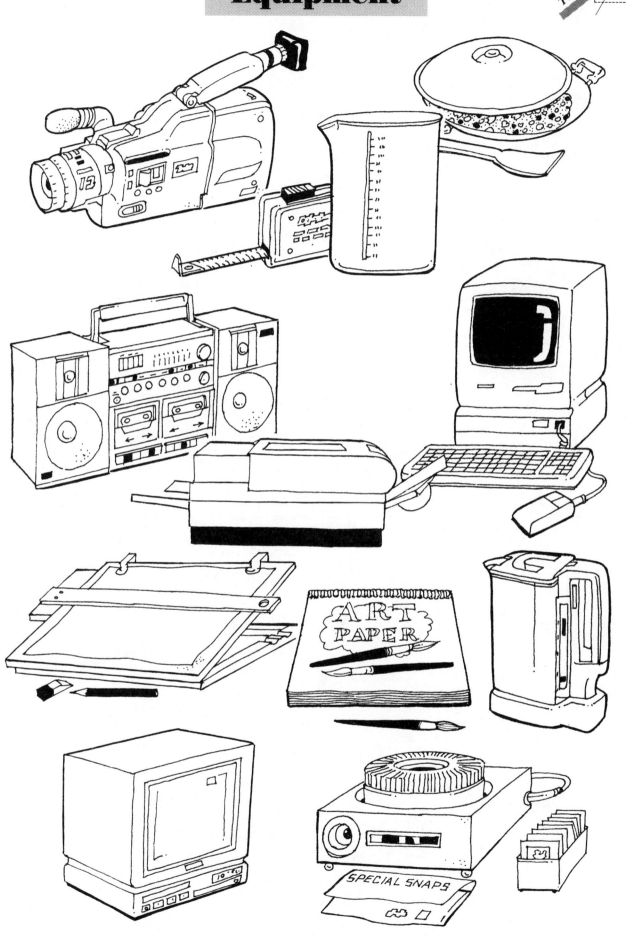

Materials

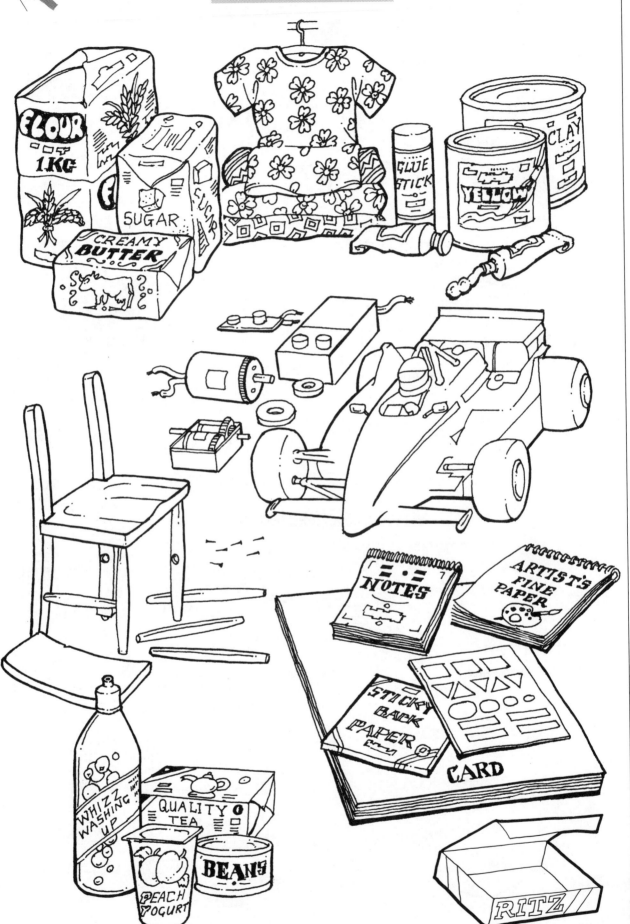

Heinemann Educational *Technology Investigations*

Safety

Control systems

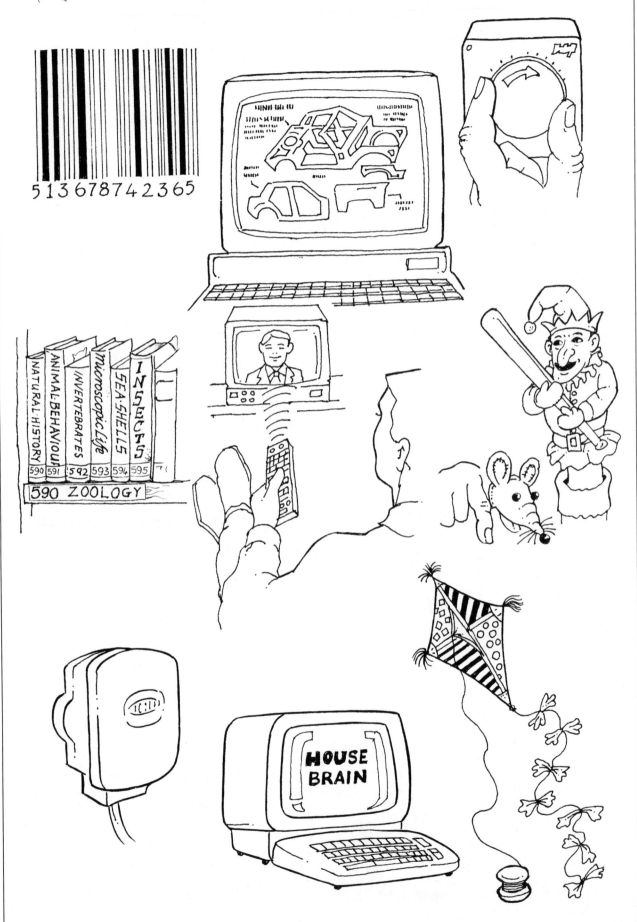

Heinemann Educational *Technology Investigations*

Mechanisms

Structures

Energy

Generating a design proposal

Planning and making

Heinemann Educational *Technology Investigations*

Modelling

OUR MODEL MADE FROM A PLASTIC BAG

PAPER PROTOTYPE

CARDBOARD MODEL

WONDERPACK

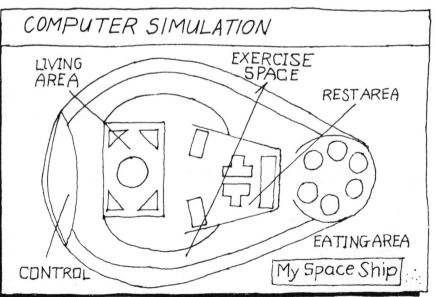

COMPUTER SIMULATION

LIVING AREA

EXERCISE SPACE

RESTAREA

CONTROL

EATINGAREA

My Space Ship

Heinemann Educational *Technology Investigations*

Evaluating

Definitions of words

The statements below are one person's idea of the meaning of the important words used in Technology.

Artefact An object made or designed by people, for example, a coat, a toy.

Coming up with a design proposal Exploring and investigating design ideas, deciding which one you are going to use and saying what you are going to do.

Control systems A set of objects or activities, which are controlled by people to help them carry out tasks; for example, a supermarket computer system, a library Dewey system.

Energy Power which may be controlled by nature or people; for example, exercise, wind power.

Environment Surroundings made by nature or people; for example, a rain forest, a bedroom.

Equipment Anything which can be used to help when designing and making; for example, a photocopier, a drill.

Evaluating Looking at your own and other people's designs and objects and thinking about how well they work.

Material The stuff which is used to make things; for example, wood, paper, fabric.

Mechanism A system of moving parts which together do something; for example, a wheelchair, a clock.

Modelling A way of testing out your ideas and presenting your designs. You can use materials such as, wood, plastic, and cardboard. A computer program can be used to make a model on the screen. Examples of models include using LEGO to make a model robot.

Need Something which is required or wanted; for example, a game to play, better food.

Planning and making Organizing time, materials and equipment and then making the thing that has been designed.

Safety Ways of working which protect people from danger, for example, using a microwave oven safely.

Structure An arrangement of parts in a construction; for example, a dog kennel, a cake.

System A set of objects or activities which perform a task, for example, a queue, a timetable.

Discuss and record

1 What do *you* think each word or phrase means?
   Use the Triggersheets to help.
   Discuss and record your own statements for these words.
   Add examples of your own.

2 What do you think is meant by 'Technology'?
   You could show your ideas in:

   ◆ drawings and sketches

   ◆ words

   ◆ a poster display

   ◆ something you have made.

Heinemann Educational *Technology Investigations*

Fact

Trapped on an island

by Nicole Obe (aged 12)

For homework Nicole wrote about being stranded on an island. Read her work and then answer the questions below.

I was stranded on an island. I was hungry and thirsty so I started to search for food and water. I hadn't gone far when I found some wild berries growing on a bush. Small birds were eating them so I knew they weren't poisonous. As I searched for water, two wild pigs came rushing towards me. I quickly climbed up a tree to avoid being trampled to death.

When they had gone I climbed down and carried on looking for water. After I had been walking for a few minutes, the ground under my feet got muddy so I knew that there was water nearby. I stood still and listened, then walked in the direction of the sound. I went down a small bank and there in front of me was a small river. I drank as much water as I could but I was still feeling hungry so I decided to try and catch some fish. I carefully placed my hand in the water and waited for a fish to come along. Finally a big trout came so I put my hand under its body and tickled its tummy. Then I flicked it out of the water and on to the bank. I got a sharp stick and took the scales off the fish. Then I made a fire by striking two flints together

over dry wood and cooked the fish. After eating it I decided to try and get off the island. First I wrote a message on a piece of bark and tied it to a bird. I hoped that someone would find the message.

It was getting late and I was very tired so I gathered up some leaves and moss to make a bed. I then made another fire to keep any wild animals away.

When I woke up I felt the sun's warm rays on my back. I decided to make a small boat but first I needed some tools. I made an axe out of a big piece of flint and a strong stick. I decided to use a big log that was washed up on the shore to make my boat. After cutting all the branches off the log I carved a big hole in the top of it. I burned out the middle so that it was hollow and shaped the inside of the log so that I could sit in it. I put a small seat in it and made a pair of paddles out of bamboo sticks. I made the outside of the boat smooth by rubbing a piece of bark over the log. The boat took about two months to make. I was then able to escape.

Questions

Technology is about coming up with designs to solve people's needs.

1   Nicole was hungry and she needed food. What did she design and make to solve this problem? Evaluate her idea – would it work? Suggest improvements.

2   What other problems did Nicole face when she landed on the island? How did she solve each problem?

3   Write your own story about being stranded on an island. What will you need to do to keep alive? How will you solve these problems?

4   Design something to help you survive on your island. Sketch and label your design.

Evaluate

Amber also thought about being stranded on an island. She sketched a design to purify water on her island. Sea water was poured through an animal skin and clear water dripped into a coconut shell. Would her design work?

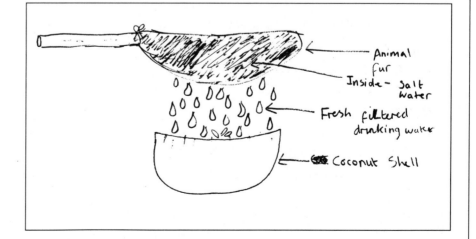

Animal fur

Inside – Salt water

Fresh filtered drinking water

Coconut Shell

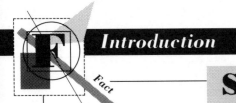
Some real designs

The designs for inventions can be **patented** or **copyrighted** in order to protect the idea from being stolen or copied. Inventalink is a company which introduces inventors and their designs to people and companies in industry, to see if any of them are prepared to produce the design for sale. You could 'phone them on 071 323 4323 to find out more about their work.

Here are some design ideas which were registered in 1991.

Cat nap video
Relieves the boredom of cats kept indoors

Finger tip implement
Restores writing ability to people with disabilities

Car security anti-theft lock
Locks the front seat to make it impossible to drive away

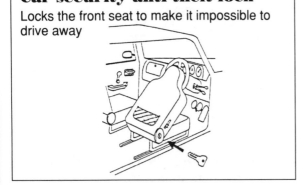

Bread keeper and dispenser
Fresher bread – on a spring

Evaluate

Use role play to evaluate these designs. Work in groups of 4–5.

Imagine that the inventor of one of these designs has to present the idea to a group of people from industry, to see if they would like to produce the design.

Choose someone to play the role of the inventor, who explains the design to the group. You need 2–3 others to play the roles of the members of the group from industry, who ask questions about the design. One other person takes notes about what is happening. Here are some questions, to start you off.

- ◆ How does the design work?
- ◆ Who will use it?
- ◆ Who will buy it?
- ◆ How much will it cost?
- ◆ Where will it be sold?

From the answers which the inventor gives, decide whether the design will be made for sale.

Afterwards, record what happens.

Heinemann Educational *Technology Investigations*

More inventions

Here are some more designs to evaluate.

BLOW-UP LOO
To take anywhere with you

FREE! Puncture Repair Kit

ROSE-TINTED SPECTACLES

Adjustable for all head sizes
Built-in Blinkers
Built-in Illumination

NO MORE GREY DAYS

WASHABLE PAPER TOWELS

CLEAN AND AVOIDS WASTE
GOOD FOR THE ENVIRONMENT

DRIER/DISPENSER UNIT

USED TOWELS

WASHER/SMOOTHER/JOINER UNIT

Evaluate

Evaluate these designs. You could:

◆ Act out a scene between the designer and someone thinking of buying the design.

◆ Write a short report to explain the good points of the design and why it might not be a success.

◆ Carry out a survey to find out what other people think of each design.

Further work

1 Design your own crazy invention. Create an advertisement to help it sell and ask others for their comments.

2 Design your own cartoon sketch to show why your crazy design was needed and how it developed.

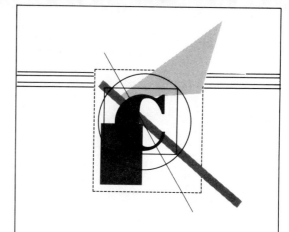

CARROTS

Bugs Bunny

Carrots are used to tell jokes!

Did you know?

In 1990 Bugs Bunny, the cartoon character famous for eating carrots, was 50 years old. Since Bugs became a star he has eaten thousands of carrots, in 180 films. After his first films were shown, people began to copy him – eating more carrots.

The Utah Celery Company of Salt Lake City offered to keep all the staff at Warners' film studio supplied with celery for the rest of their lives if Bugs would switch to celery.

The Broccoli Institute had a try, too, but it was no good. Carrots were Bugs's trademark.

Why does he chew carrots so much? Bob Clampett, who directed many of the early films, says, 'It's an old trick. It saves Bugs rushing from one joke to the next too quickly.'

Source: *Daily Mail*, 28 May 1990

Design a funny sketch

In a group, make up a funny sketch which lasts about five minutes. You could use Bugs's trick of pausing after each joke.

Discuss

- ◆ What topic will you choose?
- ◆ Will you write a script or use a storyboard?
- ◆ How will you make it funny?
- ◆ How will you present your funny sketch to others?
- ◆ Will you perform to an audience? Or make a video? Or an audio tape?
- ◆ Could you use a computer program to make an animated cartoon?

Evaluate

Present your design and ask other people for their comments.

Heinemann Educational *Technology Investigations*

Statements of attainment
Te 1/3a, b; **Te 2**/3b, c; **Te 3**/3a, 6a; **Te 4**/3a

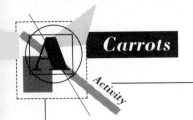

Storyboards

A storyboard is one way to show how something can be done. It shows the order of events – a **sequence**. Putting things into order helps you make sense of the process and organize what has to be done. As you learn to make plans, you are **designing** a new **system** for managing your work. Storyboards are used for cartoons, tape slide shows and making videos. They help with planning these activities.

On this page is an example of a storyboard which a primary child drew to show how he made some cakes.

Design and make

Work in pairs to design and make a storyboard to show how a sandwich is made. Show what equipment you will need, and what ingredients. Then show in stages what you do to make the sandwich. Then you can follow the pictures to make the sandwich. Use the cake-making storyboard on the right to help give you ideas.

Evaluate

You can both evaluate the storyboard and decide how easy it was to follow. Suggest ways it could be improved.

We bake some cakes

First we washed our hands

Then we turned the cooker on

we got the equipment that we needed

We used flour, butter, sugar and eggs to make our cakes

we put a cherry in the top and we took them home to eat

Heinemann Educational *Technology Investigations*

Storyboards for videos

A well-made video needs to be planned ahead before filming starts. Video producers use **storyboards** to show what the different sections of the film will contain. The storyboard helps you to think clearly about the purpose of the film and reminds you of what you have to do when you are out on location.

This storyboard has been designed for a booklet for the Comic Relief Video Relief Challenge to help pupils plan out a 3–5 minute video. It shows what has to be filmed, and the sounds and voices which need recording.

SCENE	SPEECH	SOUND EFFECTS
	Presenter: This is the XXX Day Centre. Pensioner's groups use it. It is under threat of cuts	Traffic passing
	Interview group of OAP's about their clubs, etc... and campaign to save the Day Centre	Background chatter
	Campaign in action	Street sounds
	Local councillor: campaign will be discussed at upcoming council meeting	
	Outside town hall on day of meeting. Decision to save centre	Traffic passing
	Talking to OAP's celebrating their victory	Background of party and celebrations

Source: Comic Relief/Charity Projects Education Department

Imagine that you have to use this storyboard to make a 5 minute video with your group.

◆ How much time will you give for each of the 6 scenes shown on the storyboard? Remember the total time is 5 minutes.

◆ Interviewers make a list of **key questions** – important things they must ask during filming. For scenes 2 and 6 write a key question to ask the group.

◆ How easy is this storyboard to film? What problems might you face? How could you adapt the storyboard to make filming easier?

Statements of attainment
Te 3/4e; Te 4/3a

Storyboard

Picture

Description
_____
_____
_____
_____

Speech
_____
_____

Sounds
_____

Picture

Description
_____
_____
_____

Speech
_____
_____

Sounds
_____

Picture

Description
_____
_____
_____

Speech
_____
_____

Sounds
_____

Heinemann Educational *Technology Investigations*

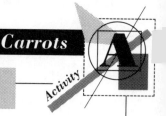

Designing a storyboard

Design and make

Design and make a storyboard – you could design your own idea for a video, cartoon or computer animation program. Look at the example from Comic Relief, on Activity sheet 51. Limit your storyboard to 6 scenes. Ask others for their comments.

Evaluate

Collect examples of storyboards. Cartoon strips will do. Show them to members of your group. Do you think the storyboards work well?
Record your findings.
You could use ideas from your storyboard collection to help with your own storyboard designs.

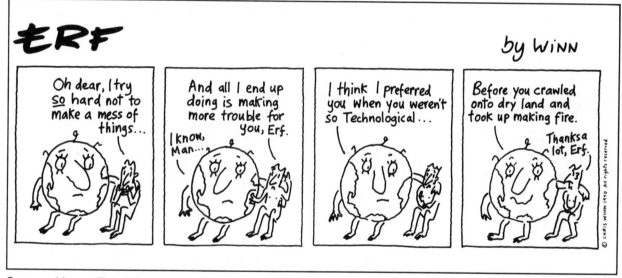

Source: *Young Telegraph*/Chris Winn, 24 November 1990

Discuss and Record

◆ Where will the action take place?

◆ Will you use just pictures, pictures and words or pictures, words and sounds?

◆ How many frames will you use?

◆ What is going to happen?

◆ Will you use real people or cartoon characters?

You can use the blank storyboard on Activity sheet 52 to help. Ask others to evaluate your design and suggest improvements.

Heinemann Educational *Technology Investigations*

Statements of attainment
Te 1/3a, b; **Te 2**/3c, 4a, 5c; **Te 3**/4b; **Te 4**/3a

Carrots in wartime Europe

The Second World War was a time of great food shortages, both in Britain and Europe.

In Britain a campaign was started to encourage people to 'Dig for Victory' and grow more of their own food. School playing fields and parks became allotments where green vegetables, potatoes and carrots were planted.

Soon there were so many extra carrots that the government launched a campaign to get people to eat more of them. The campaign used characters such as Clara Carrot and Doctor Carrot to deliver the message. War torn Poland suffered severe food shortages and a Polish recipe book of the day, written by Zofja Nowosielska, was full of recipes for sweet and savoury dishes using carrots.

One popular dish for a trifle contained grated carrot. The quantity of each ingredient is very small because food was in short supply during the war.

POLISH WARTIME COOKERY BOOK

ZOFJA NOWOSIELSKA

Carrot and apple trifle

Ingredients
2 digestive biscuits
100 g grated carrot
150 g grated apple
10 g sugar
30 g sultanas
200 ml ready made custard

Method
Crumble the biscuits and place in a small dish.
Mix the carrot, apple, sugar and sultanas and place on top of the biscuits.
Cover with the custard and leave to set.

CHEESE ROLL AND SALTED CRACKERS

CARROT CHEESE ROLLS

½ teacupful finely grated Carrot	2 teacupfuls Flour
½ teacupful finely grated Cheese	3 teaspoonfuls Baking Powder
	2 tablespoonfuls Lard
	1 teaspoonful Salt

Mix flour with baking powder and salt. Add carrot, cheese and lard. By hand make pieces of dough into thin rolls 3 inches long. Dredge baking tray with flour. Place little rolls on it. Brush rolls with milk. Bake in moderate oven 20 minutes.

TREFOILS

½ teacupful finely grated Carrot	1 tablespoonful Margarine
1½ teacupfuls Flour	2 teaspoonfuls Baking Powder
1 tablespoonful Lard	1 teaspoonful Salt

Mix flour, salt and baking powder. Add carrot and fats. Knead well. Take pieces of dough and roll them by hand into pencil shapes 12 inches long. Double; leave loop at top. Twist ends a little, then turn ends up, right and left, into the loop. Thus forming a trefoil.

Place on tray dredged with flour. Brush with milk. Bake in moderate oven for 20 minutes.

NOTE.—Before baking, trefoils may be sprinkled with salt, maw (poppy seed), or cumin.

Heinemann Educational *Technology Investigations*

Food rationing and health 1

Design and make

In wartime Britain there was a glut of carrots, and people needed to keep healthy. Newspapers and magazines encouraged readers to make special carrot recipes such as Portman Pudding, given below.

What could you design and make to use this glut of carrots and help people to keep healthy?

Research

- ◆ Find out what is meant by a 'healthy diet'.
- ◆ What foods were **rationed** during the Second World War?
- ◆ Find out more about food campaigns during this war. You could visit the Imperial War Museum in London, or your local museum may have exhibits from the Second World War.
- ◆ What tasty, healthy carrot recipes could you make using the ingredients available in wartime Europe?

Evaluate

Plan and test your ideas. Do they taste good? Are they healthy? You could compare your recipes with those used in wartime.

Portman Pudding

6 ozs. flour, 4 ozs. each grated raw carrot and potato. Teaspoon mixed spice, 2 table-spoons sugar. Level teaspoon bicarbonate of soda, pinch of salt. ¼ cupful of sultanas and raisins, 2 ozs. fat. Cream fat and sugar, add carrot, potato, flour, spice and soda. Mix well together. Add fruit. Add water if necessary to make a stiff dropping consistency. Steam for 2 hours at least. Serves 3 or 4. A sweet that needs little sugar!

© Crown copyright

 MINISTRY OF FOOD

GROW fit not fat on your war diet! Make full use of the fruit and vegetables in season. Cut out "extras"; cut out waste; don't eat more than you need. You'll save yourself money; you'll save valuable cargo space which is needed for munitions; and you'll feel fitter than you ever felt before.

PLAN YOUR MEALS THE 4 GROUP WAY

Choose something from each of these four food groups every day. Remember that the cheaper *energy foods* such as potatoes and bread give more energy than meat; that green vegetables and salads are among the best *protective foods*; that milk is the best of the *body builders* and also a valuable *protective food*.

BODY BUILDING FOODS	ENERGY FOODS	PROTECTIVE FOODS	
		(A)	(B)
Milk	Potatoes	Milk	Potatoes
Cheese	Bread	Butter	Carrots
Eggs	Flour	Margarine	Fruit
Meat	Oatmeal	Cheese	(fresh or canned, but not dried)
Fish	Rice	Eggs	Green
	Sago	Herrings	Vegetables
	Sugar	(fresh, canned or salt)	(fresh or canned, but not dried)
	Dried Fruit	Salmon	Salads
	Honey	(fresh or canned)	Tomatoes
	Cheese	Liver	Wholemeal
	Butter		Bread
	Margarine		Brown Bread
	Dripping		
	Suet		
	Lard		
	Bacon		
	Ham		

THE MINISTRY OF FOOD, LONDON, S.W.1

© Crown copyright

Heinemann Educational *Technology Investigations*

Statements of attainment

Te 1/3a, 4f, 5b, 7c; **Te 2**/3b, c, 5c; **Te 3**/3b, c, 4c, 5c, 6a; **Te 4**/4d, 5a, c, 6b

Food rationing and health 2

Evaluate

Work in groups and discuss the information given on the Ministry of Food leaflet on Activity Sheet 55.

◆ The wartime diet was said to be a healthy way of eating. What do you think?

◆ How does the wartime healthy eating message compare with those given today?

Use leaflets and books to help you.

Design

If you had to design a healthy eating campaign for wartime Britain, what ideas would you consider?

How would you deliver the message – magazines, radio, newspapers, leaflets . . . ?

Keep a record of your ideas and show how they develop.

Plan

You could ask people who lived in Britain during World War 2 to tell you about their experiences and how they managed with food shortages.

Ask them to evaluate your campaign to see if you have overlooked any problems.

10

	9	10	11	12	13	14	15
MEAT	9	10	11	12	13	14	15
EGGS	9	10	11	12	13	14	15
FATS	9	10	11	12	13	14	15
CHEESE	9	10	11	12	13	14	15
BACON	9	10	11	12	13	14	15
SUGAR	9	10	11	12	13	14	15
	P	Q	R	S	T	Q	R

MINISTRY **MF** OF FOOD

RATION BOOK

(GENERAL) 1944–45

Surname . . . .

Other Names . . . .

Address . . . .

(as on Identity Card)

NATIONAL REGISTRATION NUMBER

FOOD OFFICE CODE No.

G

R.B.1 1   GENERAL

Serial No. of Ration Book

CP

IF FOUND RETURN TO ANY FOOD OFFICE

© Crown copyright

A ration book

Heinemann Educational *Technology Investigations*

─── *Statements of attainment* ───

Te 1/3a, b, 4b, c, f, 5b, 7c, d; **Te 2**/3b, c, e, 4a, 5c; **Te 3**/4b, 6e; **Te 4**/3a, 4a, c, d, 5a, c, 6b

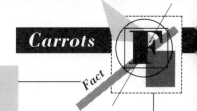
Food rationing in Britain during World War 2

Food rationing in Britain began on 8 January 1940, four months after the war had started.
Each person was allowed per week:
12 ounces (350 g) sugar
4 ounces   (100 g) butter
4 ounces   (100 g) bacon or ham

11 March   *Meat was rationed although offal – heart, kidney, liver etc. – remained unrationed.*

June 1940   *Tea was rationed to 2 ounces (50 g) a week.*
1941 was the worst year for food shortages. Many boats bringing food from other countries were sunk and there was very little choice in the shops.

March 1941   *Jams, margarine, syrup and treacle were rationed to 8 ounces (200 g) per person per month.*
Later, cheese was rationed to just 1 ounce (25 g) a week. Dried egg powder was introduced and each person was rationed to one packet every six weeks, the equivalent of 12 eggs. Children under six had two packets.
More and more land was cultivated for crops of potatoes, carrots, wheat and sugarbeet but, by 1942, more foods were rationed.

January 1942   *Dried fruit, rice, sago, tapioca and pulses were rationed.*

March 1942   *The government halted the production of white bread, to save the cargo space taken up by flour from North America. Everyone had to eat the 'National Loaf'.*

April 1942   *Breakfast cereals and condensed milk were rationed. Most people had about 2 pints of milk a week.*

July 1942   *Chocolate and sweets were rationed.*
Most people thought that rationing was a fair way of sharing the little food that was available.
Rationing in 1943 and 1944 remained about the same. Peace in 1945 brought little change in the food situation and food continued to be rationed for several years.

In recent times, the wartime diet has been recognized as a good, healthy way of eating.

Heinemann Educational *Technology Investigations*

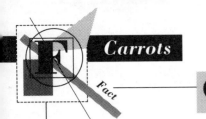

Carrots for cosmetics

Skin and hair products have been used by men and women for thousands of years. Ancient Egyptians cleaned their faces with cream made from oil and lime juice. They made perfumes from myrrh, cinnamon and oil and, if the scent was too strong, they diluted it with sweet wine. They rubbed carob on their bodies as an antiperspirant! Honey was one of the earliest skin care products. The Egyptians embalmed dead bodies in honey to prevent decomposition, since they found that bacteria would not grow in honey.

The Body Shop makes several beauty products using carrots. Carrots provide a natural filter against the sun's rays. Vitamin A, which is found in carotene in carrots, may help skin to heal.

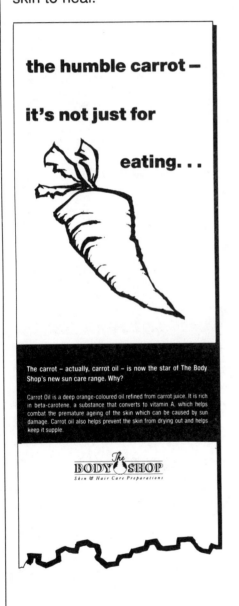

the humble carrot –

it's not just for

eating. . .

The carrot – actually, carrot oil – is now the star of The Body Shop's new sun care range. Why?

Carrot Oil is a deep orange-coloured oil refined from carrot juice. It is rich in beta-carotene, a substance that converts to vitamin A, which helps combat the premature ageing of the skin which can be caused by sun damage. Carrot oil also helps prevent the skin from drying out and helps keep it supple.

THE BODY SHOP
Skin & Hair Care Preparations

Carrot Sun Range: Introducing The Body Shop's

Carrot Sun Oil SPF 6

A low protection sunscreen body oil containing a blend of carrot and soya oils, together with cocoa butter to promote a deep even tan while keeping the skin supple.
SKIN TYPE: skins that do not burn easily, or those with an established tan.

Carrot Sun Milk SPF 12

A moderately high protection sunscreen which is light and non-greasy and easily absorbed. It contains carrot and coconut oils to help promote a smooth, even tan while keeping the skin moisturised and supple. Includes UV absorbers to screen out the sun's harmful rays.
SKIN TYPE: all types, escept fair skins that burn easily.

Carrot Sun Milk SPF 20+

An ultra-high protection sunscreen with UV absorbers to shield you from the sun's harmful rays. This is a light, moisturising lotion with carrot and coconut oils to help promote a smooth, even tan while keeping the skin healthy and supple.
SKIN TYPE: all types, especially very fair and sun-sensitive skins.

And, for after-sun care:

Carrot Soothing Gel

A clear gel which combines the soothing effect of aloe vera and the Chinese herb ginseng with the beneficial skin softening properties of carrot oil. Ideal for use after exposure to the sun, the gel will cool and soothe, leaving the skin feeling moisturised and refreshed.
SKIN TYPE: all types, including reddened, sunburnt skin.

DO NOT USE ON BROKEN SKIN.

* For more information on our Carrot Sun Care Range, refer to the Production Information Manual, available for reference in all UK Body Shops.
* For more information on all aspects of sun care, see our Customer Information leaflet, Your Skin and the Sun, available free in all UK branches of The Body Shop.

Carrot products on sale in the Body Shop
Source: The Body Shop

Heinemann Educational *Technology Investigations*

Design a cosmetic 1

> ## Design brief
> ◆ Design a skin or hair product using vegetables, plants or fruit as an ingredient.
> ◆ Make and test a recipe and design the packaging.

Research

Work in groups and brainstorm ideas.

◆ What skin and hair products are for sale which use fruits or vegetables?

◆ What do people like to use?

Record your findings.
How are new products designed in business?
Cosmetic manufacturers prepare a **product brief**. This is a statement about the product they want to design.

> We want to design a range of natural products using carrots as an ingredient. The products must fit in with our company image and use environmentally friendly packaging. They must be reasonably priced to suit all pockets. The target market is men and women from 15–55 years.

What about **product image**?
The Body Shop has a 'natural' image and likes to use natural ingredients in its products. The dictionary defines 'natural' as 'existing in, or produced by nature'. So carrots are a natural product. Think about how you could design a product from natural materials.

Design

Companies often carry out **market research** to provide them with information and ideas about people's needs.
Think up a design proposal for your skin or hair product. It should describe your product and say what you are going to do and how you are going to do it.
The proposal can change as you carry out more research.
Think about the image of your product.

Research

Decide upon your **target group** and the type of product you would like to make.
If you designed a **questionnaire** you could find out what skin and hair products your target group uses and likes. Their replies could help with your design ideas.

Heinemann Educational *Technology Investigations*

Statements of attainment
Te 1/3a, b, 4e, 5b, 6a, 7b, c; **Te 2**/3a, b, c, e, 4a, b, d, 5a, c, e, 6a, 7a; **Te 3**/3b, 4b

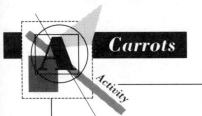

Design a cosmetic 2

Plan and make

What type of product will you make?

You need to try out several recipes and test them out on your target group.

How will you design a test? Use Factsheet 61 to help.

Record how you choose the best idea.

How will you pack your product?

Think about: the shape of container you could use.

A computer program can help you with design ideas.

What materials will you choose for packaging?

Factsheet 69 will help.

What about the label and logo? Use Factsheets 70 and 71 for ideas.

Investigate how much it will cost to make, and decide upon a selling price. What extra costs do manufacturers need to add on in order to make a profit?

Did you know

A newspaper article investigated the cost of a bottle of perfume and discovered that:

- ◆ basic ingredients cost 10%

- ◆ packaging, distribution and marketing cost 45%

- ◆ 15% is paid to the government in tax

- ◆ 30% is profit divided between the shops and makers.

What materials can we use?

How will we test it?

Is it safe to use?

Discuss, evaluate and record

In a small group, discuss how you might test your cosmetic product to make sure it is safe to use.

Draw up a company policy to show how your group will test your product. Explain why you have come to that decision.

Evaluate

How does your product compare with others for sale in the shops? If you were able to use the equipment, materials and technology available to industry, what improvements could you make? Record your ideas.

Heinemann Educational *Technology Investigations*

Statements of attainment

Te 1/3a, b, 4b, 5b, 6c; **Te 2**/3b, c, e, 4a, d, 5a, 6a, 7a, b; **Te 3**/3b, c, 4b, c, 6a; **Te 4**/3a, b, 4a, b, c, d, 5a, 6b

Views on animal testing

In one of their leaflets, against testing on animals, the **Body Shop** says:

There are three main types of animal testing.
1 Toxicity *Substances are tested to see how poisonous they might be. A group of animals is force fed large quantities of a substance, such as lipstick, until half of them die. Rats and mice are used for this test.*
2 Eye irritation *Products such as shampoos are tested by dripping or spraying them into rabbits' eyes. The amount of damage to the eyes is measured.*
3 Skin irritation *Animals such as guinea pigs and rabbits are shaved and products such as deodorant or face cream are taped on and left, to see the reaction.*
The figures
- ◆ *In 1989, 14 000 animals were used in experiments to do with cosmetic products.*
- ◆ *7100 experiments involved applying substances to the eyes of rabbits.*

Different views

Cosmetic companies must be sure that:
- ◆ customers can use products without harmful effects
- ◆ factory workers are safe when they handle products.

Some companies think that other tests are not reliable.

People who represent the animals believe that:
- ◆ innocent animals should not suffer for people's vanity
- ◆ animals do not respond to tests in the same way as humans
- ◆ some tests are badly designed
- ◆ there are other ways of testing cosmetics.

ISSUES

Animal testing and cosmetics

C R U E L
U N N E C E S S A R Y
R E J E C T E D B Y
T H E B O D Y S H O P

The Body Shop's view

How does The Body Shop address this issue?
- ◆ They use ingredients such as honey and beeswax which have been used for hundreds of years.
- ◆ Many ingredients come from plants which are used as food – so they have been tested by being eaten!
- ◆ Staff who work for the company act as volunteers for testing.

What other ways of testing are being developed?
- ◆ Computer analysis is used to predict how the new product will behave.
- ◆ In vitro tests – animal cells from dead animals are used.
- ◆ Bacteria can be used for tests.

Heinemann Educational **Technology Investigations**

Statements of attainment
Te 1/3a; **Te 2**/3b, c

What is on a cosmetic label?

The cosmetic industry has to follow laws on labelling. By law, the container and packaging of a cosmetic product must show:

◆ the name and address of the manufacturer

◆ a 'best before' date if the product cannot be stored for long.

Other information which can be found on a label includes:

◆ a logo

◆ the name of the product

◆ ways to use it

◆ description of the contents

◆ the quantity in the pack

◆ special information.

Design

Design your own skin and hair product label.

The law for cosmetic products

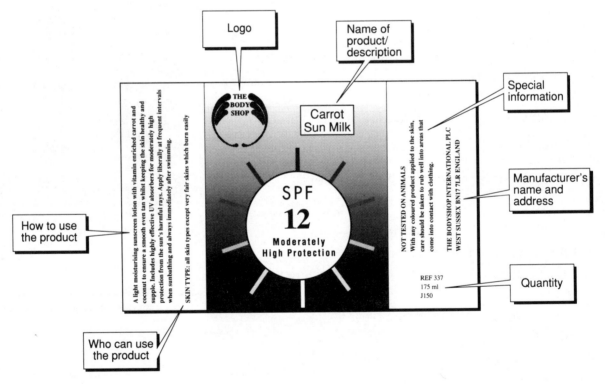

What's on a label

Use the label shown above to help.
Make sure you have included all the information which is necessary.

Statements of attainment
Te 1/3a; **Te 2**/3b, c

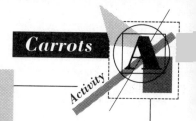

Packaging design – environmental issues

When you are designing the packaging for your cosmetic product, think about the effects it might have on our planet.

Aerosols

Supermarkets now stock ozone-friendly sprays such as hair spray. These sprays do not contain CFCs – **chlorofluorocarbons**. CFCs are gases which are used to push out whatever is inside an aerosol. They are thought to be mainly responsible for destroying the **ozone layer**.

Ozone is a gas which is found 15–30 miles (25–50 km) above the surface of the Earth. It protects us from harmful ultraviolet rays from the sun. In 1985 scientists discovered that a giant hole had appeared in the ozone layer, near the South Pole. As ozone is destroyed, more of the sun's rays will get through, causing more people to develop skin cancer, and destroying other forms of life.

Packaging

Many things we buy have far too much packaging.
Cosmetic products may be packed in bottles, then boxes and wrapped in cellophane. Is it all necessary?

Body Shop policy

We respect the environment: we offer a refill service in our shops, all our products are biodegradable, we recycle waste and use recycled paper where possible.

Research

Carry out some research to find out about the different types of packaging used for a range of cosmetics. You could draw up a chart like the one below and decide whether the packaging is 'environmentally friendly'. Alternatively, you could enter the information on a computer database.

Product	How is it packed?	Is it environmentally friendly?

Heinemann Educational *Technology Investigations*

Statements of attainment
Te 1/3a; **Te 2**/3c, 4a; **Te 4**/4c, 6c

63

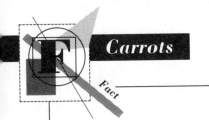

Databases

Databases are computer software programs used to input, store, sort and retrieve information. Databases work like a filing system. Information or data is entered under headings, called **fields**.

The information in the database can be easily added to and updated. It can also be sorted and analysed. Pie charts, pictograms, histograms and frequency diagrams can be drawn to show or compare data.

An advantage of using a database rather than other filing systems is that large amounts of information can be easily and quickly handled at any one time.

Some examples of database programs are:

◆ Grass

◆ Quest

◆ Key

◆ Our Facts.

Using a database – an example

Details of different accidents were collected and entered into a database program. The first column shows some of the **fields**.

```
O   AGE      :  10
O   PLACE    :  KITCHEN
O   TYPE     :  BURNING
O   INJURY   :  SCALDS
O   BODYPART :  HAND
```

These printouts were produced.
This is a **histogram** to show the numbers of accidents according to age.

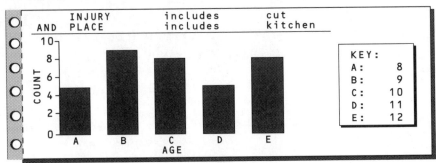

```
     INJURY        includes      cut
AND  PLACE         includes      kitchen
```

KEY:
A : 8
B : 9
C : 10
D : 11
E : 12

This **pie chart** shows the types of cut which might happen in the kitchen.

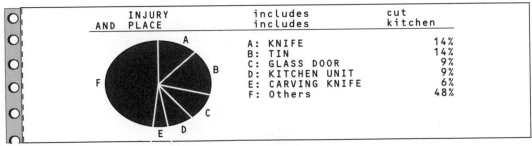

```
     INJURY        includes      cut
AND  PLACE         includes      kitchen
```

A: KNIFE   14%
B: TIN   14%
C: GLASS DOOR   9%
D: KITCHEN UNIT   9%
E: CARVING KNIFE   6%
F: Others   48%

Heinemann Educational *Technology Investigations*

Creating a database

Pupils from Hillingdon set up a database containing information on animals. The information was sorted to show the food they eat.

The **venn diagram** shows how many animals eat meat and are nocturnal. The **pie chart** shows the skin coverings different animals have.

We wanted to record some facts about animals. We began the 'Animals' file by thinking of headings to give the computer. Information with facts about animals was added. We had nine headings, below with an extract from the file.

> These headings are called 'fields'

Wild/tame
Food
Habitat
Enemies
Countries
Groups
Nocturnal/diurnal
Covering
Markings

```
File: Animals
ANIMAL        Wild/tame   Food        Habitat    Enemies
BADGER        WILD        OMNIVORE    WOODLAND   MAN
MOLE          WILD        CARNIVORE   UNDERGR    OWL
HEDGEHOG      WILD        CARNIVORE   COVERDGR   VEHICLES
BAT           WILD        CARNIVORE   AIR        OWL
FOX           WILD        CARNIVORE   WOODLAND   BOBCAT
TIGER         WILD        CARNIVORE   FOR. JUN   MAN
PANTHER       WILD        CARNIVORE   JUNGLE     MAN
BLUE WHALE    WILD        CARNIVORE   WATER      KIL.WHAL
GORILLA       WILD        HERBIVORE   JUNGLE     MAN
ELEPHANT      WILD        OMNIVORE    JUNGLE     MAN
POLAR BEAR    WILD        CARNIVORE   ICE        MAN
JAGUAR        WILD        CARNIVORE   JUNGLE     MAN
ZEBRA         WILD        HERBIVORE   PLAINS     LIONS
```

Print a pictogram showing the different types of food animals eat.

Herbivore ■ ■

Carnivore ■ ■ ■ ■ ■ ■ ■ ■ ■

Omnivore ■ ■

How many animals eat meat *and* are nocturnal? Name these animals. Print a venn diagram.

	FOOD	NOCT/DIURN
HEDGEHOG	CARNIVORE	NOCT
MOLE	CARNIVORE	NOCT
FOX	CARNIVORE	NOCT
BAT	CARNIVORE	NOCT

Print a pie chart showing the different coverings animals have.

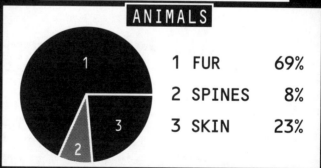

ANIMALS

1	FUR	69%
2	SPINES	8%
3	SKIN	23%

13 ANIMALS

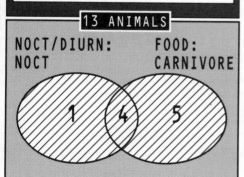

NOCT/DIURN:
NOCT

FOOD:
CARNIVORE

1   4   5

We answered a question about animal coverings. First of all the computer told us that nine animals had fur, two animals had spines and three animals had skin. We then printed out a pie chart which showed us as percentages how the animal coverings in the data-base were divided.

Packaging 1

Designers and manufacturers believe that packaging influences what we buy. This is why so much time and money is spent on package design.

People are increasingly concerned about the type and amount of packaging used. They are putting pressure on manufacturers to think more carefully about the amount of materials they are using.

The articles on this sheet and Activity sheet 67 are concerned about these issues.

Discuss and record

1 What problems does the journalist think are caused by excess packaging?
2 What can shoppers do to avoid buying extra packaging?
3 Why have McDonalds decided to change their packaging?

Packaging that costs shoppers £6 a week

CONSUMERS are paying up to 74p in the pound for throwaway packaging which poses a major pollution threat.

Manufacturers charge higher prices for wrapping a wide range of products from basic foods to luxury cosmetics, a *Daily Mail* investigation has found.

Identical baskets of eight vegetables bought at a supermarket cost £6.83 loose but £9.57 in synthetic wraps.

Organic produce and other items intended to attract the 'green' consumer were packaged in the least environment-friendly way.

And yesterday the marketing men were accused of 'taking shoppers for a ride' with appalling consequences for the environment.

Julia Hailes, co-author of the best-selling *Green Consumer Guide*, condemned the use of plastic, paper, glass and metal as 'fantastic waste'. Six million tons were discarded in Britain last year, much of it litter.

Consumer experts estimate that the average £40 bill for a family's weekly shopping includes £6 for wrapping.

Producing it not only causes pollution but also uses vast quantities of energy and materials. Disposal in tips costs £720 million a year.

It can lead to chemicals escaping into soil or the atmoshere and spreads disease among birds.

A *Mail* survey at Sainsury's found carrots in a polythene bag cost 56 per cent more than loose. Button mushrooms were 74 per cent dearer in a plastic tray than loose.

Oranges were 36p per lb loose or 45p in a string bag, nectarines 76p or 99p in plastic and garlic £1.48 or £1.89 when packaged.

Instant coffee worked out at 3p a cup in a small jar, but nearly 15p wrapped in disposable plastic cups. Toothpaste was £1.09 in a tube or £1.25 in a dispenser

WHAT THEY COST

Price per lb	Loose	Packaged
Carrots	25p	39p
Button mushrooms	£1.35	£2.36
Mange tout	£1.75	£2.48
Dwarf beans	69p	£1.07
Large mushrooms	£1.35	£1.60
English leeks	78p	89p
Parsnips	48p	59p
Baking potatoes	18p	19p

Bought at a Sainsbury's store

**By SEAN RYAN
Environment Correspondent**

Source: *Daily Mail*,
12 September 1989

The Big Mac boxes clever in cardboard

THE Big Mac will never seem the same again.

The world's most famous hamburger is swopping its distinctive foam box packaging for a cardboard container as McDonald's bows to pressure from customers and environmentalists.

The U.S.-based fast-food chain yesterday announced plans to phase out foam packaging in its 11,400 restaurants around the globe.

Cardboard packs will start appearing in American outlets over the next six months. And it won't be long before they reach Britain.

McDonald's said the move was part of a 'comprehensive' environmental initiative by the firm. President Ed Rensi claimed scientific studies showed the present CFC-free foam packaging was environmentally sound but added: 'Our customers just don't feel good about it'.

Source: *Daily Mail*,
2 November 1990

Heinemann Educational Technology Investigations

Statements of attainment
Te 1/5b; **Te 2**/3c; **Te 4**/4c, d, 6c

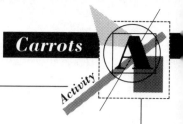
Packaging 2

Overpacking

Packaging protects goods from being damaged before you buy them and helps keep foodstuffs hygienic and fresh.

Packaging is often necessary for labelling and information.

Manufacturers sometimes use more packaging than they really need. In our survey, 4 out of 5 people agreed that too much packaging is used.

Gift wrapped luxury items, such as chocolates, use several layers of wrapping, often just to make the product look attractive.

We have picked out products which could use less packaging.

1 Sturdy plastic bottles are sometimes put in cardboard boxes. The boxes may help with displays and packing, but similar products are not packed in this way.

2 Sometimes items in boxes are also wrapped up. Herbal teas are packed in tea bags, then in a paper wrapper then in a box.

3 Multipacks such as snacks and sweets often result in waste packaging.

4 Blister packs are used to sell strong items such as toothbrushes. They help the shop to display the goods, but the packaging is not really needed.

Source: Which? magazine, August 1990

Discuss and record

Read the extract above from the Consumers' Association magazine, *Which?*, about overpacking.

1 Why do manufacturers want to use extra packaging? Give three reasons.

2 What problems might shops and shoppers face if the packaging was removed?

Research

Carry out your own survey of items which seem overpackaged. Use the illustrations below for ideas. Try to identify why the extra packaging has been used. Suggest improvements.

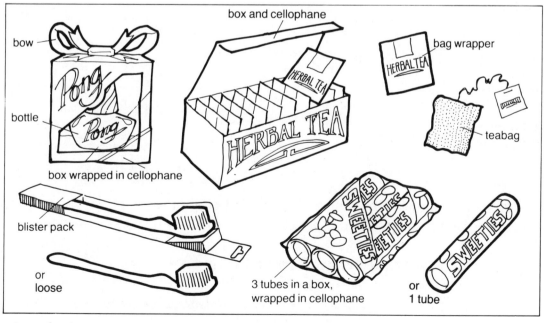

Elaborate packaging

Statements of attainment
Te 1/3a, 4b, e, 5b; **Te 2**/3c, 5c; **Te 4**/4c, d, 6d

Heinemann Educational *Technology Investigations*

Design and make your own carton

Research

Carry out some research to get ideas first.

Make a collection of cartons which hold different goods.

Use 3-D sketches to show the shape of *three* of your cartons.

Record what each carton holds and what materials are used to make it.

Take the cartons apart carefully and examine them.

Make a drawing of the carton plan or **net**.

Show how the carton fits together.

Ideas for cartons

Design and make

Use your research and Factsheet 69 to give you ideas for the design of your carton.

◆ Make a quick sketch of the design and net.

◆ Draw up a net for your design on centimetre squared paper.

◆ Make a model to test if this design will make a carton.

◆ Make changes if necessary.

◆ How will you fix the carton together?

◆ What materials and equipment do you need to make your carton?

Decide on the size of your carton.
Make up your carton and test whether it will hold things.
Ask other people for their comments.

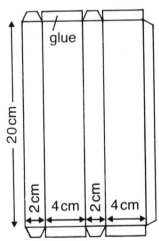

Making a carton

Evaluate

Write a short report showing the stages you went through and the changes you made when designing and making your carton. Discuss how well your design works.

Further work: printing and labelling the carton

How could you print the carton with a label and information? Try using a computer program to design patterns and shapes, and to make repeat labels to use on the sides of the packets.

Statements of attainment

Te 1/3a, 4b, e; **Te 2**/3b, c, d, 4a, b, d; **Te 3**/3b, 4e, 6a; **Te 4**/4b, c

Heinemann Educational *Technology Investigations*

Design a carton

A carton is made from **board** which is printed then folded into shape.
Cartons are good for packaging products because:

◆ they are quite cheap and easy to make

◆ they are strong and protect products from damage

◆ they can be delivered flat to factories and then made up when needed, which saves storage space

◆ they come in many shapes and sizes.

Who invented the first carton?

In 1870 a printer and bag maker from America, Robert Gair, discovered a method to crease and cut cardboard in one operation. The cardboard could then easily be folded into a carton.

The process of making a carton

Sheets of board are printed with the outline. The shape is stamped out and creases for folds are marked.

The carton can be folded and glued together.

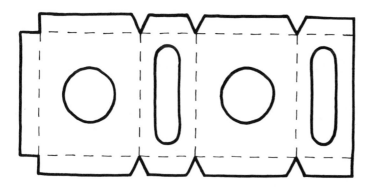

A **net** is the flat plan for the design of a carton such as a box. Here is the plan for a triangular shaped carton which fits together by folding.

Packaging net

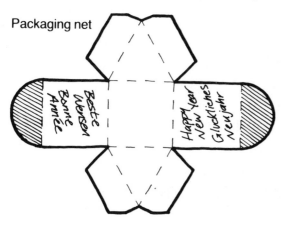

Squared paper can be used to help design a net for packaging.
Or you could use a computer program.

Heinemann Educational *Technology Investigations*

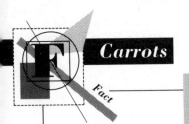

Herbie – a marketing case study (1985)

Problem

In North Yorkshire the number of pupils taking school meals had fallen. The Local Authority had to find out why.

Market research

Research was needed to find out what was wrong with the present school meals system. A **questionnaire** was designed. Here are some examples of the statements the Local Authority asked the pupils to think about in the questionnaire. The replies come from the **target groups** – year 7 and year 10 pupils.

STATEMENTS		REPLIES			TARGET GROUP
	AGREE STRONGLY	AGREE	DISAGREE	DISAGREE STRONGLY	
Should be more salads and healthy foods (fewer burgers and chips)	15	4	1	–	Year 10
Should use brown bread	6	3	3	3	Year 7
Food should be less greasy	13	7	–	–	Year 10
Chips and other foods should be less greasy	13	2	–	–	Year 7
Should be more choice of fruit and vegetables	14	4	2	–	Year 10
Should be more for afters, especially fruit	12	3	–	–	Year 7

We want less greasy, less fattening food and more fruit. Portions should be fair.

We want more choice, including vegetarian foods and snacks.

We want somewhere nice to sit.

We want well cooked, hot food made from good quality ingredients.

We don't like queueing.

The kitchens should be hygienic.

Food should look attractive and the prices should be fair.

The plan

As a result of the research findings North Yorkshire's school meals system was completely reorganized. The Local Authority drew up a plan to follow.

◆ New healthier menus have been introduced.
◆ Fresh, good quality food, with fewer additives, is used.
◆ There is a wide choice of meals.
◆ More food counters have reduced queueing.
◆ Dining areas are bright with attractive colours, fast-food style tables and chairs and the latest pop charts and radio as background music.
◆ A character called Herbie is used to promote school meals.

Heinemann Educational *Technology Investigations*

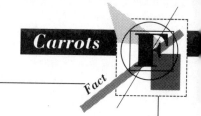

Who is Herbie?

The North Yorkshire Local Authority decided that a healthy eating campaign was needed, so that pupils knew how to make good food choices.
Herbie the carrot was designed to promote it. This name stands for 'Healthy Eating, Really Better In Every way.'

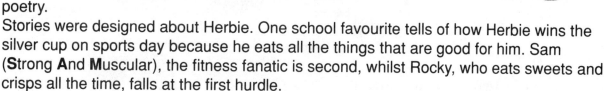
HERBIE'S HERALD

The Magazine of North Yorkshire's Education Catering Services   Autumn 1987

Lots of Herbie products were designed, including stickers, toys, games, T-shirts, mugs, posters and magazines.
There were Herbie competitions such as painting, stories and poetry.
Stories were designed about Herbie. One school favourite tells of how Herbie wins the silver cup on sports day because he eats all the things that are good for him. Sam (**S**trong **A**nd **M**uscular), the fitness fanatic is second, whilst Rocky, who eats sweets and crisps all the time, falls at the first hurdle.

The outcome

As a result of the Herbie campaign the percentage of pupils taking school meals in North Yorkshire rose from 23% in 1984/5 to 55% in 1990.
Two hundred extra people have been given part-time employment. The North Yorkshire Local Authority has won many business awards. Herbie has been a success.
It is important that the Herbie campaign continues to grow and evaluation takes place.
Here is what the Herbie campaign organizers say about evaluating the project:
'You need to find out what your customers think about you now.'

Herbie makes economic sense

Heinemann Educational *Technology Investigations*

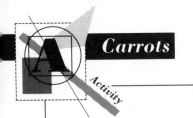
Herbie competitions

Below is a competition designed for the Herbie Campaign. Try it out for yourselves. Think up some ideas for your own competition. You could draw a kitchen or eating area showing safety hazards, for example.

Across

1. National Advisory Committee for Nutritional Education.
2. Where Herbie puts his healthy eating message across.
6. The kind of fat we should increase in our diet.
11. A healthier variety of bread, or pastry, or scone.
12. Where all things natural come from.
15. Each one.
16. The kind of oil from which Flora margarine is made.
17. Some like their steak cooked this way.
18. Preposition
20. Trend, the new Craigmillar product, is this.
24. A fruit similar to a lemon.
26. Eating healthily will give us good . . . . . .
27. A margarine which is high in polyunsaturates, low in saturates and low in cholesterol, which is now sold in portions.
28. A new Craigmillar product which is low in fat, and high in polyunsaturates.

Down

2. A fat which is harmful and should therefore be reduced in our diet.
4. Committee on Medical Aspects.
5. A prepared mix which is high in fibre and for which recipes are available in Herbie's Herald.
8. The kind of energy emitted from the sun.
9. We are full of this if we eat healthily.
10. The way to cook chops.
13. Girl's name.
14. Sounds like shortened version of you are.
16. The healthiest way to cook vegetables.
19. A wise bird.
21. We should increase this in our diet by eating wholemeal bread, fruit, vegetables and pulses.
22. The great English drink.
23. Old fashioned
25. A frying medium
26. Cooked meals should always be served in this condition.

Heinemann Educational *Technology Investigations*

Statements of attainment
Te1/3a; **Te 2**/3b, c, 4a

School meals design ideas

Use the Herbie case study to give you ideas about how to improve your school meals system.

You could design a questionnaire to find out what children think about the school meals system. What do they want changed?

Interview the school meals staff. Find out how hot food is prepared and how food is bought.

Use different ways of recording ideas:

◆ notes

◆ tapes

◆ videos.

Look at school meals systems in the past or from other countries.

Has the food changed in recent years?

You could interview teachers, parents and grandparents to get information.

SCHOOL MEALS 50 YEARS AGO/QUESTIONNAIRE

1. Did you have school meals? ....

2. What foods did you have? ....

3. Who cooked the meals? ....

Use your research to help you plan improvements to your own school meals system.

These menus are from a French lycée

Heinemann Educational *Technology Investigations*

Statements of attainment

Te 1/3a, b, 4b, f, 5a, b, 6c, 7a, b, c, d; Te 2/3b, c, 4a, 5c; Te 3/3c; Te 4/3a, b, 4b, 5b, 6c, d

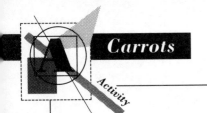

Designing patterns

Design and make a repeat pattern using a carrot

Wrapping paper, wallpaper and printed fabrics are often designed with **repeat patterns**.
There are many ways to produce a repeat pattern.
Investigate using carrots!

Research

What types of material can you print on?

◆ paper
◆ fabric
◆ wood . . .

What colour or colours will you choose?
What paints can you use?

◆ water based paints for printing on
  paper
◆ transfer paints
◆ fabric paints . . .

What equipment do you need?

◆ board
◆ sponge
◆ knife
◆ other tools . . .?

How will you cut and use the carrot for
printing? The illustration gives ideas.
Look at Factsheet 75 to give you ideas.

across

diagonally

lengthways

Ways of cutting a carrot for printing

Test out your ideas

◆ Hold the carrot in different ways.
◆ Try different processes such as rolling the carrot along the material.

Plan and make your repeat pattern

You need to find out how long the paint takes to dry.
Some fabric paints need to be **fixed** by pressing the fabric with a hot iron.

Evaluate

Discuss and compare your work with others. Explain the decisions you made about your
work and how you produced your design. Learn from what other people have done. Do
they have different ideas that you would like to use?
How could your design be used in other ways?

◆ clothing
◆ wrapping paper
◆ heading for notepaper . . .

Sketch some ideas.

─── *Statements of attainment* ───
Te 1/3a, 5b; **Te 2**/3b, c, 4a, c; **Te 3**/3b, c, 4c, 5b, c, 6a, b, c; **Te 4**/3a, b, 4b, 5b, 6c, d

Heinemann Educational **Technology Investigations**

Printing

Carrots can be cut across or diagonally to give different shapes.

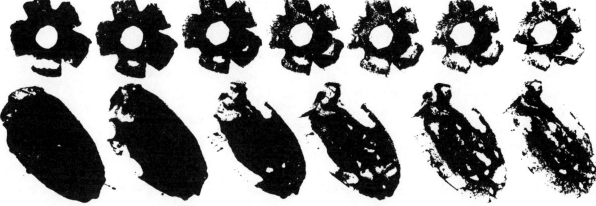

Cut the carrot into different shapes for printing.

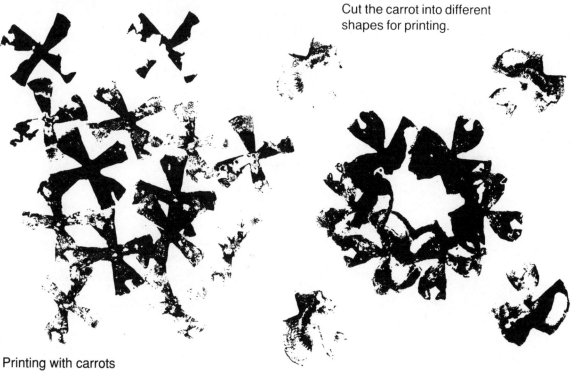

Printing with carrots

Heinemann Educational *Technology Investigations*

Carrots and your health

How to fend off a killer with carrots

Fit food

If you were not told in your youth that carrots would help you see in the dark then you probably weren't forced to eat your crusts (for your hair) or finish up your cabbage. However, if you did swallow this nutritional legend, it should now be more rewarding to discover that your early reluctant efforts at carrot crunching may have paid remarkable dividends. Carrot extract has been widely tested as an anti-cancer agent for more than 20 years and not only on small furry laboratory animals, but on human specimens too.

Dr Shekelle's research involved a 21 year study of 2000 men and concluded 'a diet relatively high in beta carotene, the chemical found in carrots and dark green leafy vegetables, may reduce the risk of lung cancer even among persons who have smoked cigarettes for many years'. He recommended a half cup of carrots a day to prevent lung cancer.

Source: *Scotsman*, 16 March 1990

Grasp a carrot

Eating carrots is not only likely to reduce the risk of certain cancers, it may also lower the risk of heart disease, says a recent report. By eating just two carrots a day you can reduce cholesterol levels by up to 20% because of calcium pectate, a form of fibre they contain.

Source: *Cosmopolitan Health Reports*

Carrot News

Britain is the second largest consumer of carrots – France being the largest. We now eat about 30% more carrots than we did 10 years ago.

Eating vegetables gives us about one third of the required daily intake of vitamin A – 14% comes from carrots. Lack of vitamin A results in dry skin and lower resistance to disease. Carrots also contain vitamin C which is needed for good health.

What are carrots made of?

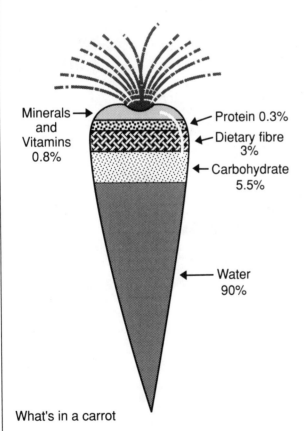

Minerals and Vitamins 0.8%
Protein 0.3%
Dietary fibre 3%
Carbohydrate 5.5%
Water 90%

What's in a carrot

Vitamins cannot increase IQ

Sales of vitamin pills rocketed two years ago when it was reported that vitamin pills decreased aggressive behaviour and boosted IQ. In a trial involving 225 North London pupils, researchers from Kings College, London, said that vitamin supplements have no effect on intelligence. A spokesperson said, 'Parents should not dose children with vitamins to raise IQ levels. The answer is to provide a sound diet.'

Botham to face Essex

WORCESTERSHIRE all-rounder Ian Botham will prepare for his comeback against Essex on Saturday on a strict diet of carrots and water.

Botham is included in the Worcestershire party who are spending three days this week at a health farm in Bedfordshire. The England star has made good progress since his knee opereation a fortnight ago.

Source: *Colchester Evening Gazette*, 16 May 1990

Heinemann Educational *Technology Investigations*

Design a health food

Design and make

Are carrots really healthy?

Your group is the **marketing team** for a company called Bozos. You have been given the task to present a **feasibility study** on the value of carrots and other vegetables as a health food. If you decide that eating more carrots is a good thing, then Bozos wants you to develop a new health food made from carrots or a mixture of vegetables which they will make.

What is a marketing team?

Companies use marketing teams to help them develop new products. The team carries out **research** to find out about products for sale. They then ask technologists and designers to develop a new product and design packaging and advertising.

What is a feasibility study?

A study is carried out to find whether or not an idea will work. Companies carry out feasibility studies to decide whether they will take on a new idea.

Carrot juice

Carotene is converted to vitamin A by the human body. It is important for the growing process, and helps towards a natural healthy complexion. Children may be given 2–3 tablespoons daily, adults may drink a glass several times a day.

Evaluate

Factsheet 76 has extracts from articles written about the health value of carrots.
Use the information to decide if you think it is a good idea for people to eat more carrots and other vegetables as a health food.
Record your findings.
Use other sources of information to help. You could use:

◆ nutrition books

◆ health magazines

◆ health shops

◆ experts such as dieticians.

Plan and make

Prepare a feasibility study to show if your team thinks carrots should be used for a health food.
Present your study to others to see if they agree with your ideas. If they give the go ahead, then decide what health food you could make.
Find out what health foods, using fruits and vegetables, are for sale. You could copy one of these ideas or invent your own.
Make your health food and test it out on others.
Ask for their comments and make changes if necessary.
Prepare a factsheet which could be sent to magazines explaining the good points of your new product.

Heinemann Educational **Technology Investigations**

───── *Statements of attainment* ─────
Te 1/3a, 4d, e, 5a, b, 6a, 7a, b, c, d; **Te 2**/3c, e, 4a, d, 5c; **Te 3**/3b, c, 4b, 6e; **Te 4**/6b, c

Cooking with carrots

The British Carrot Growers Association produces leaflets for the public which contain up-to-date information and recipes. The recipes below come from one of its leaflets.

NEW RECIPES WITH **CARROTS**

BRITISH **CARROTS** GOOD AS GOLD

HEALTHY **CARROTS**

Carrot & Chicken Stir Fry
Ingregients

150g (6oz) chicken breast, skinned and thinly sliced
5ml (1tsp) white wine
2.5ml (½ tsp) fresh ginger juice (chopped root ginger
covered with boiling water and strained)
2.5ml (½ tsp) cornflower
45ml (3 tsp) vegetable oil
100g (4oz) British Carrots, peeled and thinly sliced and blanched
1 green pepper, de-seeded and cut into strips
1 red pepper, de-seeded and cut into strips
8 tinned baby sweetcorn, halved lengthwise
5ml (1tsp) spring onion, coarsely chopped
pinch of salt and sugar
15ml (1 tbsp) white wine
Seasoning

METHOD
1. Mix together the chicken, wine, ginger juice and cornflour.
2. In a large frying pan or wok, heat the oil.
3. Stir fry the carrots, peppers, and sweetcorn. Remove, drain and keep hot.
4. To the pan add the chicken and spring onion, stir fry until the chicken is cooked.
5. Return the vegetables to the pan or wok. Add the wine, salt and sugar to taste. Serve immediately.

Serves 4.

Spagetti Carrotese
Ingregients

300g (12oz) spaghetti
75ml (5 tbsps) olive oil
6 British Carrots, peeled and thinly sliced
salt and freshly ground pepper
225g (½ lb) tomatoes, skinned and chopped
45 ml (3 tbsps) fresh basil finely chopped
Garnish
60g (2½ oz) grated Parmesan Cheese

METHOD
1. Cook the spaghetti in boiling salted water until soft. Drain and keep warm.
2. Heat half the oil and sauté the carrots over a high heat until cooked. Add the chopped tomatoes. Season and stir in the basil.
3. Add the spaghetti and mix well.
4. Serve hot sprinkled with the Parmesan Cheese.

Serves 4.

Vegetable Carrot Bake
Ingregients

50g (2 oz) butter or margarine
450g (1lb) British Carrots, peeled and finely grated
1 courgette, grated
1 ½ ed pepper, de-seeded and chopped
1 ½ reen pepper, de-seeded and chopped
1 small onion, peeled and finely chopped
6 eggs and 30 ml (2 tbsps) fresh chopped parsley
Salt and freshly ground black pepper
100g (4 oz) cheddar cheese, grated

METHOD
1. Melt the butter in a large saucepan. Add the carrots and remaining vegetables and sauté until lightly soft.
2. Beat the eggs, parsley and seasoning together, add the cheese and stir well.
3. Pour into a greased 600 ml (1 lb) loaf tin and bake in a moderate oven 375F 190C GM5 for about 45 mins until set.
4. Leave to cool before turning out. Serve hot or cold with a chilled salad.

Carrot Curry
Ingregients

5 ml (1 tsp) oil
2 cloves garlic, peeled and finely chopped
pinch cayenne
10 ml (1 dsp) ground coriander
5 ml (1 tsp) cumin and turmeric
450g (1lb) British Carrots, peeled and sliced
100g (4 oz) cauliflower florets
2.5ml (1/2 tsp) dried green chili
50g (2oz) creamed coconut
100ml (4 fl.oz) boiling water
225g (1/2lb) tomatoes, skinned and chopped

METHOD
1. In a large saucepan, heat the oil and fry the garlic and spices for 2-3 minutes.
2. Add all the vegetables including the green chili. Stir well and fry for a further 4-5 minutes.
3. Dissolve the coconut in boiling water, add to the vegetables. Add the tomatoes and cover. Simmer for about 20 minutes.
4. Serve with cooked rice and sprinkle with toasted cashew nuts.

Serves 4.

Source: British Carrot Growers Association

Make and evaluate

Work in groups and divide the recipes between your class.
Follow the recipe you have chosen.
Have a tasting session of your own and other groups' food when it is ready to eat.
Evaluate your own recipe. Think about:

- ◆ how easy the recipe was to follow
- ◆ the quantities of ingredients
- ◆ how well the method worked
- ◆ how healthy the recipe is
- ◆ what it looks and tastes like

Do you like it?
What changes did you make?

You could use the recipe evaluation on Activity sheet 79 to help you.
Write a report on your findings.
Try designing your own carrot recipe.

--- *Statements of attainment* ---

Te 1/3a, 4e, 5b; **Te 3**/3c, 4b, c, 5c, 6a; **Te 4**/3b, 5b, 6c, d

Heinemann Educational Technology Investigations

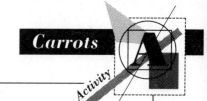
Recipe evaluation

Recipe used:	**Name:**

Evaluation

How easy is the recipe to use?

Does it work?

Suggest any changes that are needed:

How could the ingredients be adapted?

How could you make the recipe more healthy?

What did the finished dish look like?

How good did it taste?

How would you improve the recipe if you made it again?

Comments from other people who tasted the dish:

Marks (out of 10)

How easy the recipe was to follow ___/ 10

How much we liked it ___/ 10

Heinemann Educational *Technology Investigations*

─ *Statements of attainment* ─
Te 4/3a, b, 4a, 5a,b

Designs based on carrots

Carrots can be used to trigger many design ideas. Here are some things that are already for sale:

- ◆ carrot notepads
- ◆ storybooks for children based on carrots
- ◆ carrot earrings
- ◆ carrot spoons and servers
- ◆ inflatable carrots
- ◆ carrot joke cards
- ◆ carrot tea towels.

Carrot earrings

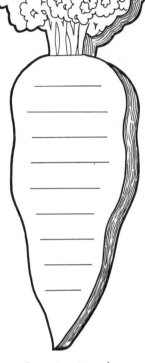

Carrot notepad

WARNING Sick Birthday Card.

WHAT'S INVISIBLE AND SMELLS OF CARROTS . . . . . . ?

DAVE.

Carrot joke card

Evaluate

Make comments on each of the designs that are illustrated.
Try and find some more examples.

Design and make

Sketch and describe your own designs based on carrots.
Try making one of them.

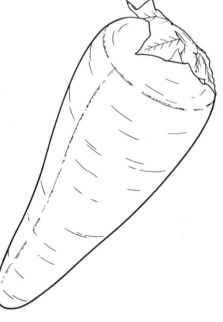

Inflatable plastic carrot

Statements of attainment
Te 2/3b, c, 4d; **Te 4**/4c

Heinemann Educational *Technology Investigations*

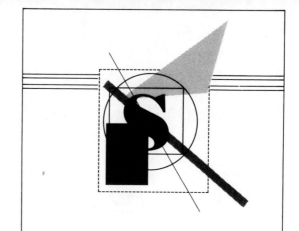

SPACE

Design ideas for a space mission

Your team has been chosen to design a spacecraft and its contents to take a crew on a 3-month mission to Zeon – a mystery planet. Funds are no problem!

LAUNCH YOURSELVES INTO THIS AND YOU COULD GO UP IN THE WORLD!

Brainstorm your team and come up with **ideas**.
Think about:

◆ the spacecraft **design** – inside and out!

◆ the **systems** which must be set up to provide for the needs of the crew.

Systems are ways in which things work.
You could design systems for:

◆ eating

◆ having fun

◆ exercise

◆ what to wear . . .

Prepare for lift off!

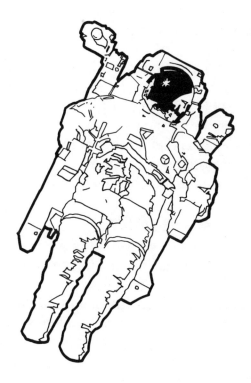

Tips

You could design plans for the whole spacecraft or just look at one system such as an exercise area.
Try making a model of your system or spacecraft.

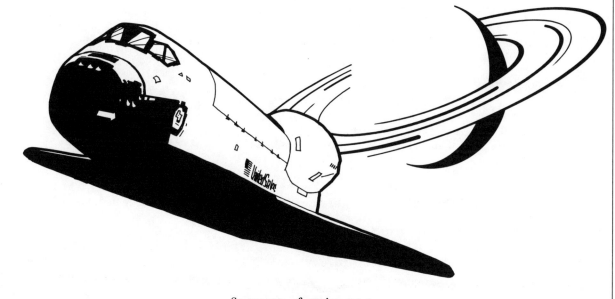

Heinemann Educational *Technology Investigations*

Statements of attainment
Te 1/4a, 6c; **Te 2**/3a, 4a, c

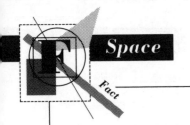

NERIS

You will need to find up-to-date information on space missions if you want to design for space. Books may already be out of date! One system you can use is NERIS, which may be found in your school or in a school or college nearby.

What is NERIS?

NERIS stands for National Educational Resources Information Service.
NERIS is an up-to-date educational information service containing over 43000 items of teaching and learning materials.
The information is stored on a CD-ROM disc which is put into a special CD player which is linked up to a computer.
You will also need a **modem** to connect your computer to NERIS via the telephone line.

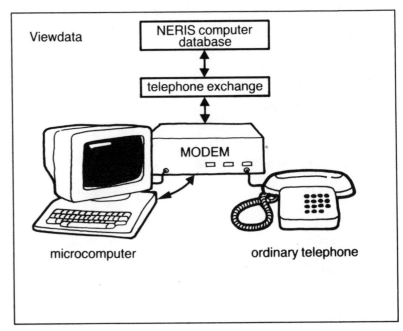

Viewdata

Why use NERIS?

NERIS saves time and the data bank is easy to use. You can quickly make a search to find the information which best meets your needs. Worksheets and project outlines can be printed out straight away.
NERIS is a good source of up-to-date material. How much information you are given varies from entry to entry. It includes books, computer software and hardware, articles, TV and radio programmes, posters, videos, etc.

```
TITLE:    MAN IN SPACE
MEDIA:    Poster; 4, 38x50cm, colour, teacher notes.
AUTHOR:   Wilson A. (Notes only)
PUBLISHER: Pictorial Charts Educational Trust (PCET)
PUBLISHED: 1983

EDUCATIONAL CONTENT:
   Showing rockets, weightlessness and the problems of living and working in
   space.
   TEXT: Extract from teachers' notes.
   EXTENSION: Complete set of notes (5pp A4).
   AGE PHASE:  11 - 16.

AVAILABILITY:
   Please use the order form which can be found in the NERIS record PCET
   ORDER FORM.
   COST: .00 inc p&p + VAT
   ORDER NUMBER: T713
   ADDRESS: Pictorial Charts Educational Trust, 27, Kirchen Road, London W13
```

Example of NERIS printout

Heinemann Educational *Technology Investigations*

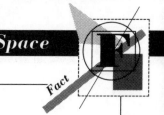

Inside a spacecraft

A spacecraft must be designed to meet several needs:
- ◆ the space travellers must be kept safe from hazards
- ◆ the craft needs to provide an environment where people can live comfortably
- ◆ people need a supply of oxygen, food and water.

What is a comfortable environment?

People need to live in an environment which has a suitable temperature and air pressure. Each person needs every day:
- ◆ 1 kg oxygen
- ◆ 0.7 kg food, freeze dried
- ◆ 2.5–3.0 litres water for drinking and washing.

The air in the spacecraft must be cleaned to remove the carbon dioxide which the space travellers breathe out.

Exercise is important in the spacecraft to keep you strong enough to return to earth. Exercise machines include:
- ◆ the **treadmill** for half an hour's walking each day
- ◆ the **exercise bicycle**.

There are also **expanders** and **springs** to help with fitness. If you are staying in space for several months you must exercise for two hours each day.

The **waste collection system** (toilet!) has a small curtain which can be drawn across, for privacy. In a weightless environment, blasts of air have to be used to carry away waste. Other spacecraft waste is either put in containers then ejected into space or taken back to Earth.

Did you know?
Floors are painted a darker colour than ceilings and walls in spacecraft? Why?
Well, when you float around you could forget you are upside-down!

Fire is one of the greatest dangers in space so all spacecraft carry fire detectors and extinguishers. Oxygen masks are kept to help breathing. You don't really need a bed in a spacecraft! You can just strap yourself into a quiet corner and sleep standing up. For extra comfort, the spacecraft has zip-up sleeping bags attached to walls or bunk beds.
You cannot take a bath on a spacecraft as your bath water would float off in droplets. Space showers have straps for your feet to stop you from ending upside-down, and water is sucked into the shower tray.

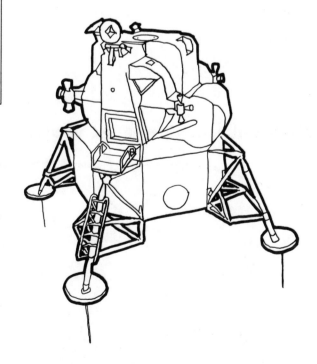

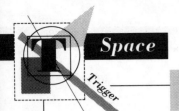
Designing a space to live

Where do people live?
Here are some ideas.
Think of others.

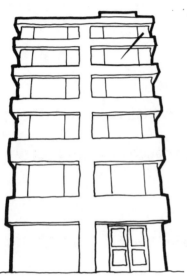

What kind of place (environment) are you designing?
Where is it to be?

- ◆ in space
- ◆ under water
- ◆ back in time
- ◆ in the future . . .?

Does your design meet people's needs?

I want to be safe

Is it warm?

Where can I eat?

I'm hot and sweaty

Where can we get some peace?

Let's read a story

You need a wash!

Heinemann Educational *Technology Investigations*

Planning a spacecraft

A spacecraft has to provide you with all you need to live during your mission.

Identify the needs

When you are planning the environment in the spacecraft you must identify your needs and those of the rest of the crew. Use Triggersheet 86 to help. Record your decisions. How can the environment of the spacecraft meet those needs?

Making plans

Sketch your ideas to show the shape of your spacecraft.
Use your sketches to help choose one design.
Label the different areas, such as 'sleeping quarters'. Do you need any special facilities?
Compare your designs with others. Add any extra ideas to your plan.
Think of ways you can present your ideas neatly.

- ◆ You could use a computer to help draw your plans.
- ◆ Do you need to learn new drawing skills?
- ◆ Do you need special graphic equipment?

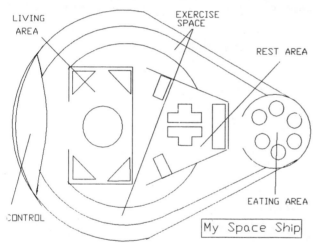

Marion drew this spacecraft using the computer program Autosketch

Design and make

What materials could you use to make a model of your spacecraft?

- ◆ wood
- ◆ metal
- ◆ paper
- ◆ fabric
- ◆ plastic
- ◆ waste materials.

Evaluation

Evaluate your work. Does the plan or model meet the needs of the crew?
Could your choice of materials be improved?
What about your method of working and the skills you used?

Statements of attainment

Te 1/4a, e, 6c; Te 2/3a, d, 4a, d; Te 3/4e, 5b, c; Te 4/3b, 5a, b, 6c, d

Heinemann Educational *Technology Investigations*

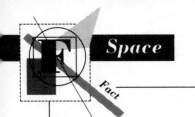
Food facts in space 1

Food on the spacecraft:
Food for space travellers must be:

- ◆ **safe** from dangerous microbes which could make people sick – food
  on space missions is **irradiated**
- ◆ **healthy** and it must contain enough nutrients to keep the space travellers fit and
  well.

Irradiation
Special energy waves are passed through the food, destroying bacteria and fungi.
Since the bacteria which make food go bad are killed, irradiated food looks like fresh
food but keeps longer. This treatment prevents the space travellers from getting food
poisoning.

Space diet
Under weightless conditions minerals are lost. Sodium, calcium and nitrogen are
important for bone strength and muscle power, so plenty of these minerals are needed in
space meals.
Here is a 12 600 kJ (3000 kcal) day's menu for a space mission.

BREAKFAST	LUNCH	DINNER
apple purée	sausages	prawn cocktail
muesli	turkey	steak
scrambled eggs	bread	rice
bran	banana	broccoli
chocolate milk	sweet bar	fruit cocktail
orange juice	apple juice	caramel pudding
		grapefruit juice

Fact box
- ✓ More than 100 different foods are available on a space mission.
- ✓ 20 different types of tea and coffee are available.
- ✓ Food is vacuum packed, dehydrated and deep frozen.
- ✓ Many foods have been dried to save weight and space.
- ✓ Real orange juice and milk are replaced by synthetic juices and skimmed milk.
- ✓ 'Natural' foods which are packed in cans or irradiated include peanut butter,
  biscuits, sweets, canned tuna fish and fruit.
- ✓ Water is available as a by-product of the system which provides the spacecraft
  with electrical power.

Heinemann Educational *Technology Investigations*

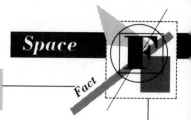
Food facts in space 2

When technologists plan food for space flights they think about how food should be stored and made hot.

The first space missions had small cubes of food and paste in bags which the space travellers squeezed. None of the food tasted very good, and crumbs floated into the instruments.

Before space missions, space food is cooked, divided into portions, then freeze dried and vacuum packed in clear packages.

Cooking in space

The **space mission galley** is where food is prepared for eating.

The crew insert the nozzle of a water dispenser gun to add water to the food in the packets.

Food can be made hot in the oven. Drinks are in closed plastic packs. When you need a drink you push a drinking straw into the pack. Otherwise, in weightless conditions, a drink would float away in blobs!

Eating meals on a tray

Food packs are held in place on trays by means of magnets or Velcro. Trays are fastened to tables by clamps to stop them floating away. There are magnets on spoons, knives and forks too!

Most food is covered in thick sauce to help it stick to the fork or spoon.

If your food floats away you can just get up and catch it in your mouth!

Cleaning up

Water will not stay in the wash basin so the galley has a special hygiene station for hand washing and cleaning up. Plates are often cleaned with 'wet wipes'.

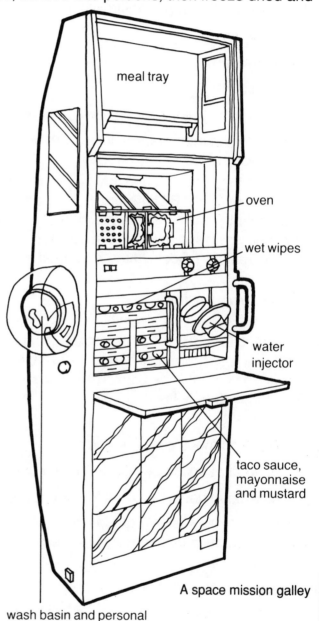

meal tray

oven

wet wipes

water injector

taco sauce, mayonnaise and mustard

A space mission galley

wash basin and personal hygiene station

Joke

What did the astronaut find in the chip pan?

An unidentified frying object!

Heinemann Educational *Technology Investigations*

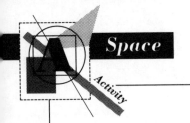
Space food

What food would you take on a space mission?
What menus would you design for the crew?

Discuss, evaluate and record

Use Factsheets 88 and 89. Evaluate the day's menu for a space mission.
Is it healthy and attractive? What you would choose?
Find out what changes would need to be made if members of the crew are:

◆ vegans

◆ Jewish

◆ diabetic

◆ have any other special dietary needs.

Use a computer program (such as the Food Program ILECC) to help analyse the value of a space menu.

In Japan they have an unusual way to try to get people to eat a healthy diet. Each person tries to eat 30 different foods a day. Invent a day's meals for a space traveller. You could try out the Japanese idea of eating 30 different foods each day.
How will you test out your menu to see if it provides a variety of nutrients and whether or not it is healthy? Does your menu need improving? Make changes if necessary.

Plan and make

Plan and cook a space meal.
You could test your ideas on others using a **tasting panel**.
Design a **questionnaire** to find out what they think.
How can your meal be packed for a space flight to save as much room as possible? Use Factsheet 89 to help.
Think about:

◆ which foods could be dried

◆ what needs to be cooked before the flight

◆ what materials you would need for packing.

Record the progress of your ideas showing how you have changed them.
You could use plans, drawings, models or flow diagrams.

Joke
What is a space traveller's favourite meal?
Launch!

Heinemann Educational **Technology Investigations**

Statements of attainment
Te 1/4a, b, e, f, 5b, 6b, c, 7c; **Te 2**/3a, b, c, e, 4a, d, 5a, c, e, 6a, c; **Te 3**/4c, e, 5b, 6a; **Te 4**/4d, 5a, b, 6c

90

Space suits

When space travellers leave their spacecraft to go into space or walk on the moon, they must wear special protective clothes, otherwise they will die.
Since there is no air to breathe in space, suits are fitted with oxygen tanks.
Space can be very hot in the direct sun, and freezing cold in the shade of planets. Spacesuits are designed with water-cooled underwear. Tubes carry water around to keep the space traveller's body temperature steady. The spacesuit even has a special nappy inside so the space traveller can go to the toilet!

Discuss and record

Look at the picture of the spacesuit. What are the special needs of space travellers when they leave the spacecraft? What features of the spacesuit are designed to meet these needs? Why are these features useful?
Discuss these questions with others then fill in the chart below to record your findings.

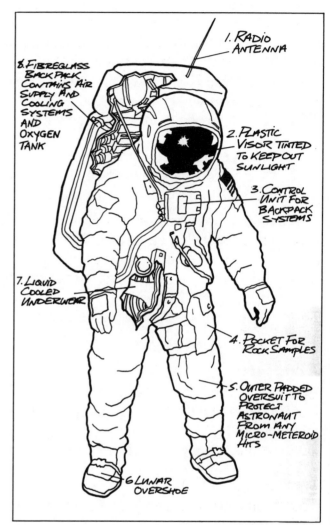

Clothes for space missions

Special design features	Why are they needed?
1. Radio antenna	to keep in touch with the spacecraft

Heinemann Educational *Technology Investigations*

Statements of attainment
Te 1/4a, 5b, 6c; **Te 2**/4a; **Te 4**/4c, d

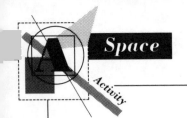

Space clothes

Although space travellers need to put on spacesuits when they leave the spacecraft, they can wear ordinary clothes inside.

When designing clothes for space travellers to wear inside the spacecraft, designers must think about the spacecraft environment.

◆ Everything floats about because of weightlessness – so skirts would float up and down!

◆ Loose sleeves or trousers would get caught in the switches and instruments.

◆ Clothes must be comfortable.

◆ On a space mission the body stretches 30–60 mm in length and muscles get smaller.

One idea that designers came up with for the Space Shuttle missions were **coveralls**. They are like a jumpsuit and are loose – but not too loose – and comfortable. They have plenty of pockets, for small items and pens which would float around otherwise.

The coverall is made from flame retardant fabric in case of fire.

The coverall

Evaluate

Evaluate the design for the coverall.

How does it meet the needs of people working inside the spacecraft?

Do you think it is a good design? Give your reasons.

Design

Your team is travelling on a space mission and you need to design a uniform to wear inside the spacecraft.

Think about the planet you are visiting – what is the environment like?

Sketch some ideas.

Record how your designs develop.

Discuss with others which design or combination of designs you will choose.

What designs did you reject and why?

How about a logo to identify team members?

Will your space clothes have any special features?

What materials can you use?

For example, you could use fabrics, metals or paper.

Evaluate

Talk to other people about your design. Discuss how you decided what was worth doing. What features of your design are especially useful?

Computer aided design of a logo

Heinemann Educational *Technology Investigations*

Statements of attainment

Te 1/4a, c, d, e, 5b, 6c; **Te 2**/3a, b, c, e, 4a, b, d, 5a, b, 6a, b; **Te 3**/3b, 5b; **Te 4**/3a, 4a, b, c, d

Clothes

How do you choose what to wear?

Purpose

Climate

Tradition

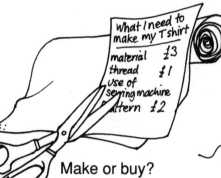

What I need to
make my T shirt

material   £3
thread   £1
use of
sewing machine
pattern   £2

Make or buy?

TO FIT HIPS
97-102cm 38-40in

100% POLYAMIDE

COOL

FLAME RESISTANT

DAZZLE CLEAN
AUTOMATIC

Safety, health and cleanliness

Fabric

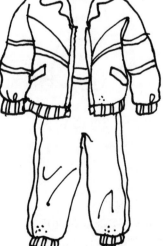

Comfort

Style: what you like

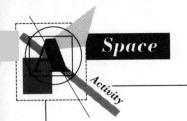
Choosing fabrics

It is important that fabrics for clothing and furnishing are chosen carefully. There are several things to think about.

How does it look?

How does it feel?

What are its properties?

Fabrics can be specially treated to change their properties

Modern technology allows fabrics to be treated with special finishes to protect them and improve quality:

◆ **for longer life**: stain resistant, water repellent, crease resistant, water proofing

◆ **for safety**: flame resistant

◆ **for easy care**: minimum iron, shrink-resistant, permanent creases, dye-fast, tumble dry.

Trendy fabric

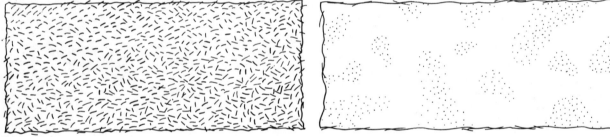

Rough

Soft

Water resistant

Stretchy

Research and record

Use Activity sheets 95, 96 and 97.

Find samples of fabric to show different properties.

Collect other samples of fabrics which show special finishes.

Design a display sheet to show the results of your research.

Statements of attainment

Te 1/3a, 4e, 5b, 6c; **Te 2**/3b, c, 4a; **Te 3**/3b, c, 4c, 5b, 6a, b; **Te 4**/4c, 6b

Fabric sheet

Looking at pieces of fabric can help you think about the properties of materials – how they feel, look and behave.
Choose four pieces of fabric from the 'bit box'.
Cut a small piece from each and stick them in the 'sample' boxes below.
Fill in the boxes beside each one.

Sample of fabric	How does it look?	How does it feel?	Describe its properties
	Words to help: colourful, pretty, trendy . . .	Words to help: soft, itchy, warm, rough . . .	Words to help: stretchy, waterproof, warm, crumples, strong . . .

Statements of attainment
Te 1/5b, 6c; **Te 2**/3b, 4a; **Te 3**/3b, c, 4c, 5b, 6a, b; **Te 4**/6a

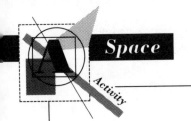
Testing fabrics 1

Before you make something using a fabric, it is useful to *test* the fabric to see if it meets your needs.

This sheet and Activity sheet 97 show some simple tests which can be carried out in the classroom.

Does it stretch?

Equipment:
pieces of fabric approximately
3 cm x 10 cm
ruler
drawing pins
wooden board

What to do:
Pin one end of the fabric to the board.
Stretch each piece of fabric and measure with a ruler.
Did the fabric spring back to shape? Measure to check.

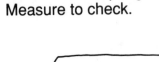

Does it shrink?

Equipment:
pieces of fabric approximately
10 cm × 10 cm
warm water
bowl
ruler

What to do:
Soak each piece of fabric overnight in warm water.
Dry the fabric.
Measure each piece to see if it has shrunk.

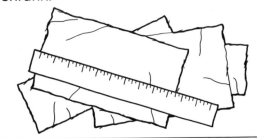

Does it wear away?

Equipment:
pieces of fabric approximately
10 cm × 10 cm
small piece of nylon pan scourer

What to do:
Rub each piece of fabric 10 times with the nylon pan scourer.
Do bits of fabric wear off?

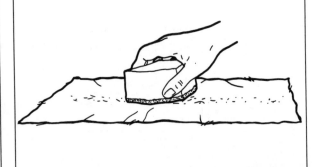

Does it soak up water?

Equipment:
pieces of fabric approximately
10 cm × 10 cm
cold water
measuring jug

What to do:
Soak the fabric in water for 5 minutes.
Squeeze out the water into the measuring jug.
How much water did the fabric soak up?

Statements of attainment
Te 1/4e, 7b; **Te 3**/3c, 5c, 6a, b, 7b

Heinemann Educational *Technology Investigations*

Testing fabrics 2

Does it crease?

Equipment:
pieces of fabric approximately
10 cm × 10 cm
What to do:
Squeeze the fabric in your hand for 2 minutes
Does it crease?
Compare different fabrics.

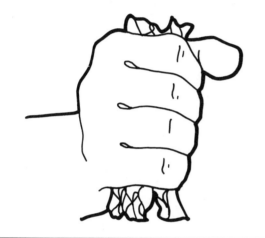

Is it resistant to water?

Equipment:
pieces of fabric approximately
10 cm × 10 cm
pipette
cold water
What to do:
Put 3 droplets of water on to each piece of fabric.
Does the water soak through the fabric?
If not, the fabric is water resistant.

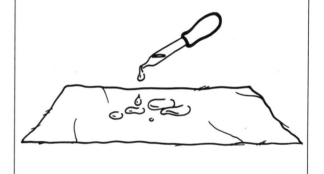

Does it keep things warm or cool?

Equipment:
4 thermometers
4 containers wrapped in fabric
foil tops for containers
hot water
What to do:
Fill the containers with 100 ml of boiling water at 100 °C.
Fit on the foil tops.
Make a hole in the foil tops and place a thermometer in each container.
Record the temperature every 5 minutes.
Draw a graph to show your results or enter the information into a computer database.

Does it catch fire?

Equipment:
pieces of fabric approximately
10 cm × 10 cm
pair of tongs
roasting tin
taper
What to do:
Pick up a piece of fabric with the tongs.
Hold it over a roasting tin for safety.
Light it carefully with the taper.
Does it catch fire?
How quickly does it burn?
Record what happens.

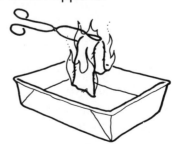

Heinemann Educational *Technology Investigations*

Designing with a computer

Computer programs can be used to draw designs for fabrics and create shapes.
Here is an example to show how a program called Drawmouse has been used to make a
fabric design which can be used on clothing.

Stage 1
Draw the design on the screen.
Choose the colours.
You could draw the design on an
acetate sheet, then stick it to the
screen and copy the design.

Stage 2
Repeat the design to make a pattern for your fabric.

Stage 1; repeat for stage 2

Stage 3
Draw an outline for your clothes.
Fill in the outline with your chosen colour.
Note: Filling in prevents the design from covering the whole screen.

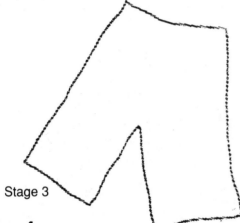

Stage 3

Stage 4
Load the fabric design on to the screen.
Reload the clothing shape.
The fabric design will now show on the
clothing.
You can print out your results.

Stage 4

Ideas

Use a computer program to help you draw your own design for a fabric and try to
create a repeat pattern.
Design some shapes for clothing and try and fit on your pattern. Experiment with
different colours on the computer screen.

Statements of attainment

Te 1/3a, 5b, 6c; **Te 2**/3b, c, 4a, d; **Te3**/3c, 4e, 6a, 7a, b

Heinemann Educational *Technology Investigations*

Designing a name and logo with a computer

Design a name and logo for the team going on the space mission. This design could be used for:

- ◆ uniforms
- ◆ bags
- ◆ letter headings.

Research

There are many types of **lettering** you can use.

Make a collection of lettering styles from newspapers, magazines and labels. Display your work.

Look at the computer programs available for your use and find examples of lettering styles or **founts**. Print out examples.

Logos

Logos are designs which help people identify schools, shops and companies easily.

Design and make

Choose a team name.

Use a computer program which has different lettering styles.

Type in your team name.

Experiment with different types of lettering and their sizes.

Choose the design you like best.

Explain why you have made this choice.

Use a computer program to design a logo.

Experiment with shapes and pictures.

Try drawing repeat images.

Try making the images different sizes.

Try using the lettering and pictures together.

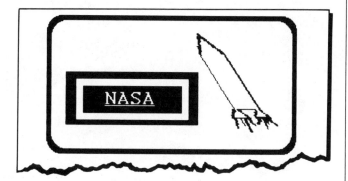

Evaluate

Print out examples of your logo.

Choose the design you like best.

Write or tape record an evaluation explaining how you came to your final choice, and how you went about the design process using a computer.

Some examples of computer software programs which can be used for this work are:

- ◆ Caxton Press
- ◆ Write
- ◆ Paintbrush
- ◆ Paintspa
- ◆ Autosketch
- ◆ Lincad

Statements of attainment

Te 1/3a, 4e, 7b; **Te 2**/3a, e, 4a, b, 5a, b, c; **Te 3**/4c; **Te 4**/3b, 4b

Space logos

Heinemann Educational *Technology Investigations*

Games in space

What games do space travellers play?
On space flights there is plenty of time to relax and play games. Games using cards or dice have to be redesigned since the lack of gravity makes things float around the spacecraft.

Darts only need to be thrown gently for them to float slowly towards the dart board. You need to attach your feet to the floor when you throw the darts, otherwise you will twirl round your own centre of gravity.

Chess and board games need magnetic pieces on magnetic boards to stop things floating around the spacecraft. Throwing dice is impossible in space since they never settle in one place. Instead, games use a mini computer which shows a random number.

Computer games are really popular on board spacecraft.

Card games are tricky since the cards will not stay on the table. Elastic bands are fitted to the centre of the table to hold the cards in place.

Space tag games Chasing someone in space is very difficult. If you hold them you tumble around together, but if you let go you will float apart again!

Ball games are great fun in the spacecraft. Balls bounce off the walls just like they would on Earth. Catching a ball is not easy, though. If you jump up to catch it you sail past the ball and miss. Balls do not move fast in weightless conditions. If you anchor yourself with foot straps then even table tennis is possible.

Designing a game in space

The crew on your space mission includes some small children. Your team needs to plan some games for them which can be taken on the flight.

Research

Carry out some research to discover which games are popular.
You could use a computer program such as Survey or Questionnaire to help.
On the right below is an example of a questionnaire designed using Survey, showing questions 2 and 4.
The aim of the questionnaire was to find out what games are popular with children of different ages. Twelve children were interviewed and the bar chart and pie chart show some of their replies.

How many people do you like to play games with?

a. None ....

b. One ....

c. Two ....

d. Three ....

e. Four ....

f. More ....

How often do you play games?

a. Every day ....

b. Every 2-3 days ....

c. Once a week ....

d. Less often ....

Examples of survey questions

Fact box
These are the ten most popular indoor games sold in Britain.

Nielson Toys' Index
12 months to May 1990

1	Trivial Pursuit	Tonka
2	Pictionary	Tonka
3	Scrabble	Spear
4	Water Games	Tomy
5	Dingbats	Waddingtons
6	Monopoly	Waddingtons
7	Blockbusters	Waddingtons
8	Heroquest	MB
9	Hungry Hippos	MB
10	The Neighbours Game	Crown & Andrews

Source: *Toy Trader Magazine*, September 1990

Do you or your friends play any of these top 10 games?
How could this list help you with your plans for games to take on a space mission?

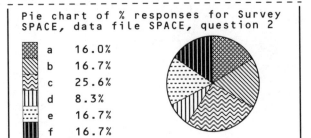

Pie chart of % responses for Survey SPACE, data file SPACE, question 2

	a	16.0%
	b	16.7%
	c	25.6%
	d	8.3%
	e	16.7%
	f	16.7%

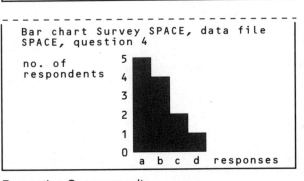

Bar chart Survey SPACE, data file SPACE, question 4

no. of respondents

Presenting Survey results

Joke
What is the space traveller's favourite game?
Astronauts and crosses!

Heinemann Educational *Technology Investigations*

Statements of attainment

Te 1/3a, 4b, 5b, 7a, c; **Te 2**/3b, c, 5c, 7a, c; **Te 3**/4c, 5b, c, 6b, c; **Te 4**/4c

Designing games

Work in a group. Divide the tasks up between you.

Research

Find out about games:
- ◆ in different parts of the world
- ◆ played in the past
- ◆ popular games played today.

Use Factsheet 101 and Activity Sheet 102 to help.

Play some games

Who are the games designed for? This the **target group**.
Are they fun to play? Why, or why not?
Present your findings to other people.

More research

Ask people what games they enjoy playing today.
You could carry out a **survey**. What questions will you ask?

WHAT'S IN SANTA'S SACK

1) **NINTENDO GAME BOY**
2) **BIKE**
3) **CAMERA**
4) **SCALEXTRIC**
5) **WORD PROCESSOR**

Source: *Daily Telegraph* 22 December 1990

What games can you design?

Use your research to generate ideas.
How many people will your game be for?
Will it be played inside or outside?

What are the aims of your game?

Will it help people to keep fit, learn a skill like counting, have fun or use a computer?
Does your game need rules?

Can you make your game?

How long will it take?
Use drawings, models and diagrams to help.
Do you need special materials or equipment?
Do you need to learn new skills?
How can you test your game?
How can you evaluate your work?

Statements of attainment

Te 1/3a, 4b, e, f, 5a, b, 6a, b, c, 7a, b, c; **Te 2**/3b, c, d, e, 4a, d, 5a, c, e, 6a, c, 7a, c; **Te 3**/4b, c, e, 6a, b, 7a, b; **Te 4**/6b

Heinemann Educational *Technology Investigations*

Design a robot

Robots can carry out many of the tasks which people find difficult or time consuming. If you are designing a robot you need to think about several things.

What can a robot do to look after people's needs?
- cleaning
- mechanical repairs
- cooking
- child care …

What uses can you think of for robots?
Record ideas by:
- drawing
- diagrams
- making notes
- using a computer.

Choose one of your ideas
Write a **design brief** to show how your robot meets people's needs. Ask others what they think of your idea.
Make changes if necessary.

Can you make your robot?
Or design a model of your robot?
Will you work alone or as a team?
How will you share the workload?
What materials and equipment do you need?
Do you need to learn new skills?
Change your plans if necessary.

Materials
How much will they cost?
Are they easy to use?
Ideas!
- packaging materials
- plastic
- wood
- fabric
- metal.
Make a list of what you need.

Equipment
What tools and special equipment do you need to make your robot?
Ideas!
- drills
- vacuum former
- saws.
Do you know how to use them safely?

Testing and evaluating
How can you test your robot?
Show your robot to others and ask them what they think.
How does it meet your original needs?
How could you improve your design?

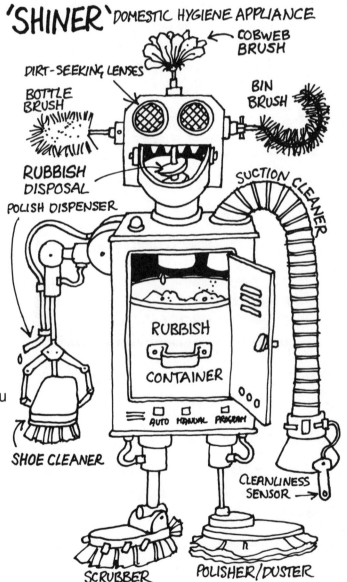

'SHINER' DOMESTIC HYGIENE APPLIANCE
← COBWEB BRUSH
DIRT-SEEKING LENSES
BOTTLE BRUSH
BIN BRUSH
RUBBISH DISPOSAL
POLISH DISPENSER
SUCTION CLEANER
RUBBISH CONTAINER
AUTO MANUAL PROGRAM
SHOE CLEANER
CLEANLINESS SENSOR →
SCRUBBER
POLISHER/DUSTER

A cleaning robot

Heinemann Educational *Technology Investigations*

Statements of attainment
Te 1/4a, 5b, 6c, 7c; **Te 2**/3b, c, d, e, 4a, b, c, d, 5a; **Te 3**/3b, c, 4b, c, 5b, c, 6b, c, 7a, b; **Te 4**/3a 5b, 6b
---

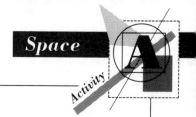

Computer robots

Some robots can be controlled using a computer.
The **floor turtle** is a pen-carrying robot which can be programmed to draw patterns using the computer language **Logo**.

The floor turtle

Design

Design your own robot which can be controlled using the computer programming language Logo.
Identify a **need** – design a robot that performs an action or task normally done by humans.
Keep a file of all your designs ideas. Include:

- ◆ plans
- ◆ flow diagrams
- ◆ notes
- ◆ drawings which show how your robot works.

Make your robot

To built and operate your robot you could use:

- ◆ Lego
- ◆ motors
- ◆ sensors
- ◆ lights
- ◆ electromagnets
- ◆ sound detectors.

Evaluate

Evaluate and make changes to your work as you go along. Find ways of testing how well your design meets the need. Make a presentation of your work:

- ◆ show other people your file
- ◆ talk about the choices and decisions you made
- ◆ discuss possible improvements that could be made to your design.

Statements of attainment
Te 1/4a, 5b, 6c, 7c; **Te 2**/3a, b, c, e, 4a, d, 5a, e; **Te 3**/3b, 4c, e, 5b; **Te 4**/3a, b, 4a, b, d, 5a, b, 6b, d

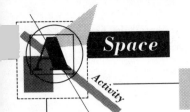

Robot Olympics

'Hello, cup,' said the voice from the loudspeaker. A robot which looked like a small suitcase had seen a mug on a computer screen.

Having seen it, the robot issued regular reminders of its intelligence to the small crowd of humans gathered at the First International Robot Olympics in Glasgow. Unfortunately there was something wrong with the suitcase robot – there was something wrong with several of the other machines on show.

Earlier, a robot called Trolleyman should have carried an Olympic torch along the street. Sadly, Trolleyman stubbornly refused to move anywhere unless he was carried by public relations men.

Inside Strathclyde University's sports hall there were javelin-throwing robots, robots that walked like scorpions, a fat, old-fashioned robot from India with 1950s wiring, and contraptions on wheels which were meant to avoid objects but kept having to be rescued from collisions.

Children from Inverkeithing Primary School, Fife, had to make their small, plastic-ball robot, clean up multi-coloured crystals dozens of times for TV crews.

Everyone agreed that robotics had not advanced as fast as had been expected. It is extraordinarily difficult, for example, to teach a machine to distinguish between a shadow and a real object.

Twenty or thirty years ago robots were totally deaf, dumb, blind and stupid. They could only be used for the simplest of tasks such as paint-spraying and spot-welding.

Now, says Dr Jim Alty, research director of the Turing Institute, which organized the Olympics, robots are hard of hearing and stagger about a lot. Their potential for doing jobs too dangerous for humans – such as repairing nuclear reactors – is huge.

Source: *Guardian,* 28 September 1990 (adapted)

Building Robots

Ruzena Bajcsy, a professor of computer science in America, aims to produce a robot that will learn to recognize objects, without having to refer to rules stored in their electronic memories. 'Rule based systems are rigid and have many shortcomings.'

To recognize a tree according to rules, the robot's memory would contain a description of a tree as an object with a trunk, branches and leaves. If a robot met a palm tree, it would not recognize it as a tree!

Robots need to move around smoothly. One student made a two-legged walking robot. He started his design with computer simulations of walking and tested his ideas with over 1000 different types of step. He then built a model of the robot to test his simulation. The finished robot is connected to a computer which decides where it should move next.

The students decided that robots are not easy to build!

Source: 'Mechanical athletes totter towards Olympic Glory', *New Scientist*, 6 October 1990 (adapted)

Discuss and record

Use the two articles to help answer these questions.

1   Do you think the robots in these Olympics are successful designs? Explain your answers.
2   How have robots changed over the last 20–30 years?
3   What problems do robot designers need to overcome to create useful robots?
4   What steps did the student take to design and make his robot? Find out other ways robots are used in everyday life.

Heinemann Educational Technology Investigations

Statements of attainment

Te 1/5b, 6c; **Te 2**/3c; **Te 4**/4c, d

Robots – do they need laws of control?

Robots are machines, which have been designed and programmed to copy the actions of humans. In some early science fiction stories, robots took over the world.
Isaac Asimov, a science-fiction writer, thought that robots should be programmed with laws to stop this happening. So he wrote 'The Three Laws of Robotics':

1 Robots must not injure human beings or allow them to be hurt.
2 Robots must obey orders from human beings except if it means going against the First Law.
3 Robots must protect their own existence except if in doing so they conflict with the First and Second Laws.

Source: *Handbook of Robotics*, 56th edition, AD 2058

Robots in space

Unmanned spacecraft are like very clever robots: they use tools to do the same kind of work that humans do. They can be programmed like robots and react to things going on around them. However, they do not usually have arms or any way of travelling over land.

Some spacecraft, such as the American Viking Lander, which landed on Mars in September 1976, look like robots. As well as the normal equipment including cameras, weather measuring sensors and radios, it has an arm which when extended out, can push a rock aside and collect a sample of soil.

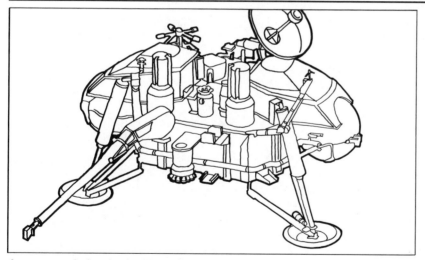

A spacecraft that looks like a robot

To do

1 Invent your own laws of robotics.
   What **constraints** or limits should be put on robots to make sure they are safe to use?
2 Carry out some research to find examples of how robots are used in everyday life.
   When do you think robots could be useful?

Joke
Why was the space robot so silly?
Because it had a screw loose.

Statements of attainment
Te 1/4a, f, 5b, 6c, 7c; **Te 2**/3c; **Te 4**/4c, d

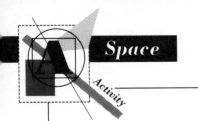

Jewellery design

Design ideas
Try making your own jewellery.

Discuss and record
Brainstorm ideas for jewellery design with your group.
Use Triggersheets 109, 110, 111, 112 and 113 to help.

Research
Here are some things to think about.
- What is meant by 'jewellery'?
- Why do people wear jewellery and body decorations?
- Is there a need for jewellery?
- Has jewellery changed over the years?
- Do both men and women wear jewellery and body decorations?
- What about animals – how are they decorated?
- Look at jewellery from other countries.
- What kinds of jewellery do you wear?
- What about older and younger people?
- Some jewellery is worn for other reasons – people who need special medical help may wear this information on chains around their necks.
- Can jewellery be useful?

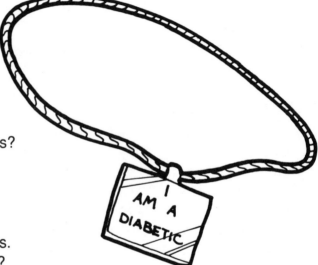

Jewellery for a special purpose

Design and make
Sketch your design ideas.
What materials can you use to make your jewellery?
Use Triggersheets 112 and 113 to give you ideas.
Do you need any special equipment?
Do you need to learn new skills?
How much will your jewellery cost to make?
Make your jewellery.

Badges are jewellery

Evaluate
Compare your jewellery with items you can buy in the shops.
How do you rate your design?
Do you think you could sell your products? How?

Heinemann Educational Technology Investigations

──── *Statements of attainment* ────
Te 1/3a, b, 4f, 5b; **Te 2**/3b, c, e, 4a, 5c; **Te 3**/3b, 4b, 5b; **Te 4**/4c, d, 5c

Jewellery

This sleeve fastener is made of gold. It is from the late Bronze Age, 8 BC.

Women in India wear very distinctive jewellery.

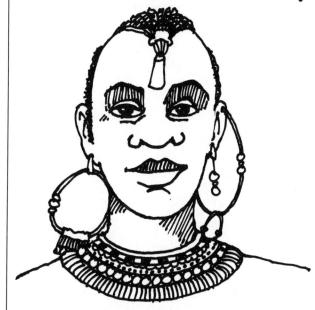

Maasai warriors wear traditional jewellery.

Pomanders contained spices and perfumes in the segments. They were worn round the owners' necks to keep away nasty smells.

Rosaries are very special forms of jewellery, used by Roman Catholics as they pray.

Jewellery for different parts of the body

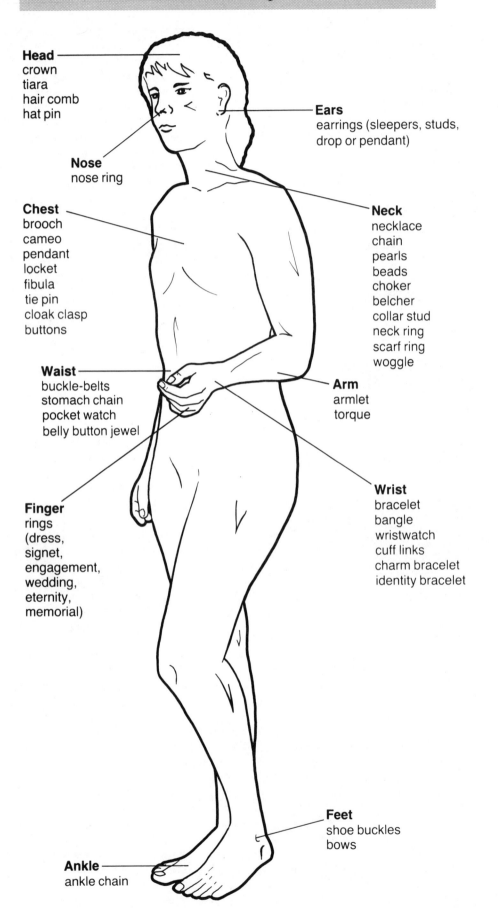

Head
crown
tiara
hair comb
hat pin

Nose
nose ring

Chest
brooch
cameo
pendant
locket
fibula
tie pin
cloak clasp
buttons

Waist
buckle-belts
stomach chain
pocket watch
belly button jewel

Finger
rings
(dress,
signet,
engagement,
wedding,
eternity,
memorial)

Ears
earrings (sleepers, studs,
drop or pendant)

Neck
necklace
chain
pearls
beads
choker
belcher
collar stud
neck ring
scarf ring
woggle

Arm
armlet
torque

Wrist
bracelet
bangle
wristwatch
cuff links
charm bracelet
identity bracelet

Feet
shoe buckles
bows

Ankle
ankle chain

Heinemann Educational *Technology Investigations*

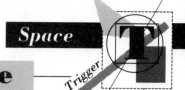

Jewellery designed for space travellers?

Here are some whacky ideas for jewellery which could be worn on a space mission.
These designs all have a dual purpose – they are useful as well as decorative.
You could try thinking up some designs, using and adapting household items such as
mini screwdrivers and fuse wire.

An **emergency oxygen mask**, looks just like
an ethnic-style head-dress with supply-pipe
neck adornment.

The **radiation survey meter ring** – changes
colour according to the atmosphere.

OPTIONAL
SOLAR
CELL

This smart **dosemeter** watch provides an
accurate record of the astronaut's radiation
intake.

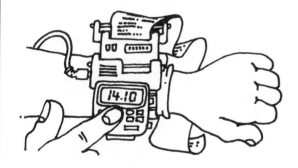

No need to check the pulse in an emergency.
This trendy **pulse sensor neck collar** gives out
an ear-piercing shriek if the pulse stops.

PRESS
TO
TEST

Pocket electronic games to keep the astronaut
active are housed in this charming **astrobelt**.

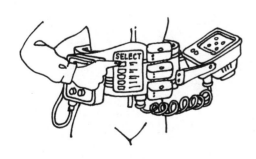

SELECT

Like leather? This **armlet** contains a
screwdriver and socket set.

Heinemann Educational *Technology Investigations*

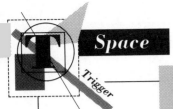
Materials that can be used to make jewellery 1

Materials for making jewellery can be found in all sorts of places.
Look around your home or studio for ideas, or go for a walk in the park. Visit your local garage or raid the fabric box.
Combine different materials for dramatic results. Spray paint a pasta spiral and you have disguised your material immediately. Try to use new and exciting ways of colouring and patterning without the usual paint and pens. You could use coloured spices or copy the colours of peacock feathers.

FOOD?
Flour   Food colouring
Pasta   Beans
Fruit peelings
Cake decorations
Biscuits

PAPER?
Papier maché
Coloured card
Origami   Printed paper
Sandpaper
Wallpaper

FABRICS?
Weaving   Knitting
Crochet
Embroidery
Plaiting   Macrami
Threads
Tartan   Stripes
Buttons   Zips
Velcro   Studs

NATURAL OBJECTS?
Stone   Mud   Sand
Straw
Precious stones
Berries   Nuts
Shells
Grass   Wood
Wool   Cotton
Glass
Silk   String
Ribbon

Heinemann Educational *Technology Investigations*

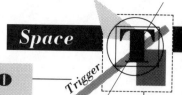

Materials that can be used to make jewellery 2

METAL?
Precious ores
Nuts and bolts
Gold   Silver   Copper
Paper clips
Mesh   Tubes

RUBBER?
Bands   Elastic
India rubber

PLASTICS?
Moulded   Glued
Cut
Jointed   PVC
Polystyrene
Clear sheets of Perspex   Beads

GLASS?
Cut   Stained
Lenses
Mirrors   Crystal

CLAY AND CERAMICS?
Plaster of Paris   Playdo
Bricks
Small Pots

Heinemann Educational *Technology Investigations*

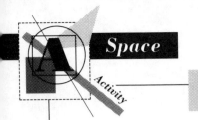
Choosing materials 1

There are many things to consider when choosing design materials. If you choose the wrong material the design may not work. Sometimes the choice is made for you and you have to make the best use of the materials available.

Here are some things which matter when choosing materials.

Environmental issues
Will it damage our environment?

Tactile quality
How does it feel to use?

Attractiveness
Do you, and others, think it looks good?

Appropriateness and fitness for purpose
Is the material really sensible to use for the design?

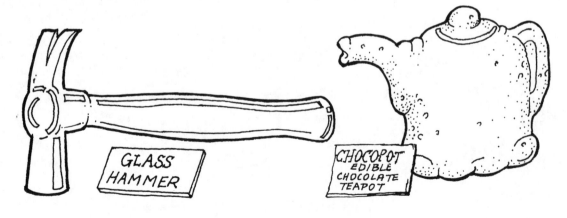

GLASS HAMMER

CHOCOPOT EDIBLE CHOCOLATE TEAPOT

Heinemann Educational *Technology Investigations*

Statements of attainment
Te 1/4f, 5b, 7c; **Te 4**/4d

Choosing materials 2

Cost
How much does it cost and will the design be worth making or sell well?

Workability
Is it easy to work and not too strong or weak? Do you have the tools and skills to handle it?

Durability
Will it last?

Availability
Is the material easy to obtain in the quantity or size you need?

Discuss and record
Make a list of each of the eight headings to think about when choosing materials. For each heading come up with some examples.

Heinemann Educational *Technology Investigations*

Evaluating materials

The designs in each of these four groups have a similar use, yet each design is made from different materials.

Discuss and record

Choose one of the groups and look at each object in that group. Think of two more examples, made from different materials. What material (or materials) has been used in each case?

Why do you think that material has been chosen for that design? You could record your findings by fllling in a chart like the one below.

Chart to show what materials are used for designs		
Design	Material	Why is it used?
rain hat	plastic fabric	because it keeps off water

Why do people need to choose different materials to make, for example, hats or chairs? To help with your answer, think about:

◆ how the objects are used
◆ who uses them
◆ when they are used
◆ why they are used.

Record your findings.

Further work

Look around for other groups of objects which have a similar use, but are made from different materials.

Examples are all around you!

Sketch and label your findings to show what materials have been used. Why do you think these materials have been chosen?

Display your work for others to see and compare ideas.

─── *Statements of attainment* ───
Te 1/3a, 5b; **Te 2**/3c, 4a; **Te 4**/4c, 6c

Heinemann Educational *Technology Investigations*

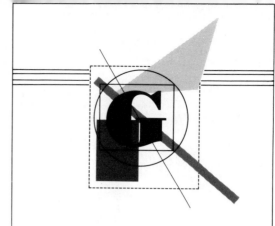

GETTING
AROUND

Safety in Technology workshops

There are many pieces of large machinery and equipment in technology workshops. Tools, machinery and equipment can all be dangerous if they are not handled properly. Before you begin to make things in Technology, you will need to understand:

- ◆ safety rules
- ◆ how to use tools, machinery and equipment.

Design brief

In industry, people have special training days to help them work safely with others in the workplace.

Your group needs to be able to work safely in the Technology area of your school. Design a **system** which you could use to deliver the safety message.

Ideas

- ◆ special safety workshops
- ◆ a video or tape recording
- ◆ displays, handouts or posters
- ◆ talks by experts.

Research

You can use Activity sheets 120, 121, 122, 123, 124 and 125 to give you ideas. Ask experts for help – your teachers.

Find out what printed information on safety is available. Explore other sources of information.

What safety symbols can you use?

Triggersheet 33 may give you some ideas.

Plan and make your system to deliver the safety message

How can you evaluate it? You could ask others for their views.

Does it meet your original aims?

Could you improve it?

Workshop safety

Statements of attainment

Te 1/3a, b, 5a; **Te 2**/5c; **Te 3**/6e, f; **Te 4**/3a, 5a, c, 6b

Heinemann Educational *Technology Investigations*

Getting around

Safety in the food area

Discuss and record

Look at the picture of the food preparation area.
How would you make this a safer place to work?
Design some rules to help pupils work safely in this area.

Statements of attainment
Te 1/3a; **Te 2**/3c; **Te 4**/4c

Heinemann Educational *Technology Investigations*

Safety in the textiles area

Discuss and record

What dangers can you spot in this textiles room?
Design a set of rules for pupils using this textiles area.

Heinemann Educational *Technology Investigations*

Statements of attainment
Te 1/3a; **Te 2**/3c; **Te 4**/4c

Safety in a multi-materials workshop

Discuss and record

Make a list of the hazards you can find in this workshop.
What improvements could be made in the way the pupils behave and organize themselves?

Statements of attainment
Te 1/3a; **Te 2**/3c; **Te 4**/4c

Heinemann Educational *Technology Investigations*

Safety in a computer area

Discuss and record

Make a list of the hazards you can find in this workshop.
What improvements could be made in the way the pupils behave and organize themselves?

Statements of attainment
Te 1/3a; **Te 2**/3c; **Te 4**/4c

Safety in an art and design area

Discuss and record

Make a list of the hazards you can find in this workshop.
What improvements could be made in the way the pupils behave and organize themselves?

Statements of attainment
Te 1/3a; **Te 2**/3c; **Te 4**/4c

Heinemann Educational *Technology Investigations*

Getting around in safety

The **environment** in which we live has many hazards.
Signs and symbols have been designed to warn us about some of these dangers.

Discuss

The pictures below show signs and symbols which meet different needs.
Discuss what you think each one means. Suggest where you might find them. Is the message always clear?

Design and make

Look around your environment. What areas need signs to warn people of danger?
Design a **system** to help people get around one of these areas safely.
Explain why you think a system is needed for the area you have chosen.
Keep a record of your ideas including drawings and plans. Show how your design has developed.

Ideas

◆ You could use rooms or machinery in your school.
◆ Think about others – is your message easy to understand?
◆ Could you use pictures instead of words?

Evaluation

Ask other people to test your system.
Make any changes that are needed.
Present an evaluation of all you have done.
Think about:

◆ whether your system meets the original need (does it deliver the safety message?)
◆ the views of people who have tested your system
◆ improvements that could be made.

Statements of attainment
Te 1/4a, e; **Te 2**/3c, e, 4a, c, d, 5a; **Te 3**/4e; **Te 4**/3a, b, 4a, 7a

Role play cards

I'm Mrs Ridgwell and this is my food preparation area. Food is a material which needs special care. It must be stored at the right temperature so it is safe to eat. Anyone working with food must be properly dressed. You must wear clean aprons, tie back long hair, remove jewellery and wash your hands before you start handling food. For safety, floor space must be clear of bags and coats, and spills need clearing up. Everyone should know how to use large equipment safely.

I'm Mrs Rutland, an IT specialist. When you come into the computer area, leave your bags and coats in the storage space before you sit down. No drinks or food should be brought into this area and there is to be no running or pushing.
Electricity must be handled safely. There should be no trailing flexes or overloaded sockets.
Make sure you have a comfortable chair, at the correct height, and work in a good light. Poor working conditions can lead to eye strain, headaches and backache.
Use the computers carefully. Some people bash the keyboard, but this can cause damage.
You need to prepare work before you use the computer, to save time. Be careful when using the discs. Save information and store work properly. Don't switch the computer off and on unnecessarily. Learn the correct 'exit' procedures.
Turn the computer off when you have finished.

I'm Mrs Harper a textiles teacher. My room is too small for everyone to have their bags and coats at their tables, so I have a cupboard where they can be stored. It stops people falling over things too. There is valuable and dangerous equipment in this room so people must behave sensibly.
We have safety rules for big pieces of equipment. For example, sewing machines must be carefully plugged into electrical sockets and not switched on until they are threaded. The classroom works better and we learn more if we follow the rules.
I expect you to leave the room tidy, so that everyone can find what they need. If you visit other areas in the Technology block please move quietly and safely.

I'm Mr Pitt, and I run a Technology workshop. If pupils are doing practical work, they must wear protective overalls, tie back loose hair and take off dangly jewellery.
Bags must be stored away from gangways. Everyone must know how to use large equipment safely. When drilling, cutting and working with hot things like soldering irons, pupils must wear goggles. We have special gloves, too. Guards are needed for high speed machinery and I must check that everything is OK before machines are turned on.

I'm Miss Lewis, an art and design teacher. Pupils need to put bags under the tables, take off their coats and wear overalls or aprons if they are working with paints, clay or ceramics. Craft knives and lino tools are sharp and dangerous. Pay attention when you are using them – do not leave them lying around.
Keep away from hot areas such as the kiln. Please tidy up brushes and paints and leave the room clean, ready for the next group.

Heinemann Educational Technology Investigations

Role play

Role play is one way of trying to understand other people.
Each person acts out the role of another character and tries to show how they would behave.
As you move around the Technology workshops, you need to organize yourselves and understand how teachers want you to behave.
Look at Factsheet 126, which records the views of five teachers who work in Technology.
Choose one of the **issues** listed below and act out what you think might happen. Use the Rules of play below.

Issues

1 A lot of pupils want to use one of the Technology workshops at the same time. The teachers are trying to explain that only a few pupils can work with the equipment. What will happen?
2 Two pupils, a boy and a girl, are having a fight beside some dangerous equipment. What will happen?
3 There is a fire in the Technology area. What will happen?

Rules of play

- ◆ Work in a group of four or five.
- ◆ Choose *one* issue to act out, and *one* of the teachers from the role play cards (Factsheet 126).
- ◆ One person takes the role of the teacher chosen and the others act out the roles of the pupils involved.
- ◆ First discuss ideas. Then run through the scene. It should last 5 to 10 minutes.
- ◆ Some ideas may work better than others – make changes as you go along if

Present and discuss

Present your play to the rest of the class. Discuss with them the issues that you have acted out and the way in which you went about the task. You may find that they would have approached the problem in a different way.

Heinemann Educational *Technology Investigations*

Statements of attainment

Te 1/4c; **Te 2**/3b, c; **Te 3**/3a, 4b; **Te 4**/3a, b, 4a, 7a

Anything can be a toy – so long as it is fun!

Discuss and record

What makes a good toy?

Triggersheet 129 shows examples of toys through the ages which all move around.

Working in a group, discuss whether the examples shown are 'good' toys.

Keep a record of your ideas – even if you do not always agree with each other.

Bring in some real toys or pictures of toys to evaluate.

Design a toy

Some toy designers watch children at play, to help them come up with ideas.

Research

Carry out an **observation** of children playing with toys. You could visit young children in a nursery school, watch younger brothers and sisters or try out some toys on members of your group. Think about these questions.

- ◆ What toys do they play with?
- ◆ How long do they play with each toy?
- ◆ What do they like or dislike about the toys?
- ◆ Is there a difference between the toys which boys and girls choose to play with?
- ◆ What age are the children you are observing?

You could draw up a checklist of points to observe, like the one above.

Add your own ideas. Your answers could be put into a database.

Planning

Write a statement describing why children need to play. Use the results of your observation to back up your statement.

Sketch some ideas for toys which move around. Your research may help you with these designs.

Design and make

Choose one of your designs to develop further, and make it.

Record how your design develops through a series of drawings. Think about:

- ◆ materials you will use
- ◆ special equipment you need
- ◆ how much it will cost
- ◆ colour and shape
- ◆ if you need to learn new skills
- ◆ the time it will take to make
- ◆ the safety of your toy – use Factsheet 130 to help.

Draw up a plan or flow diagram including this information.

Evaluation

Think of ways you could test your toy design to see if it is successful.

Statements of attainment

Te1/3a, b, 4b, f, 5b, 6a, 7b, c; **Te 2**/3b, c, 4a, c, d, 5a, d, e; **Te 3**/3a, b, 4c, e, 5b, c, 6a; **Te 4**/6b

Heinemann Educational *Technology Investigations*

Toys which go around

Safety regulations for toy design

The British Standard or European Standard Safety of Toys 1990

British and European Standards for toys state the basic requirements for safe toys. For example, toys which might be dangerous for children under 36 months of age should have a warning 'not suitable for children under 3 years'.

Toy companies use British Standards to test their products. Toys are designed to be:

◆ strong

◆ durable

◆ bright

◆ fun.

All toys should be designed with **safety** in mind.

Toy companies have specialist **toy technologists** to ensure that their toys meet the British and European Toy Safety Regulations. Some companies also follow their own strict safety standards.

Here are some of the things that toys are tested for:

◆ to make sure there are no hidden dangers such as wire sticking out, sharp edges and **burrs** – jagged plastic bits

◆ to check that children's fingers can't get trapped in toys, prams or pushchairs

◆ to ensure that teething toys are easy to clean and do not easily come apart

◆ to make sure that the eyes on cuddly toys, such as teddy bears cannot be pulled out.

Heinemann Educational *Technology Investigations*

Designing a game which goes around

Children's games have been around for hundreds of years.
Children play games in a group for lots of reasons.
Games are fun. They can play games with their friends and on cold days active games help to keep them warm.
One of the most famous traditional games is Ring-a ring o' Roses.

Design brief

Design a children's game which doesn't involve the use of extras such as balls, hoops or other objects!

Ideas

- ◆ a game in a circle
- ◆ an action game
- ◆ a clapping game.

Picture of Ring-a ring o' Roses

Source: Kate Greenaway, *Mother Goose*, Frederick Warne, 1881

Research

Ask children what games they like to play.
Find out about the games children played in the past.
Interview elderly people and use reference books.
You could use the BBC Doomsday Project interactive computer program.
Compare your two sets of findings.
When you are planning your game think about:

- ◆ what its purpose is – fun, to keep warm . . .
- ◆ who will play your game
- ◆ how many children will play
- ◆ how old they are
- ◆ where your game will be played – inside, outdoors . . .

Keep a record of your ideas and give reasons for your final choices .

Design and make

Use your research to design and make your game.
You could use plans and flow diagrams to help you.
Keep these as a record of your work.

Evaluation

Who will try out your game . . .

- ◆ young children
- ◆ classmates?

You could visit your local primary school and ask children there to play and evaluate your game.
Do they enjoy playing it?
Discuss the outcome with your classmates and teachers.

Statements of attainment

Te 1/3a, b, 4b, f, 5a, b, 7b, c; **Te 2**/3a, b, c, e, 4a, d, 5a, c, e; **Te 3**/4c; **Te 4**/3a, b, 5a

Heinemann Educational **Technology Investigations**

Games

Fantasy games
These board games allow the players to act out a fantasy story.

Pachisi
This is India's national game, and is played like Ludo.

Bocce
This is a game that was played by Ancient Greeks and Romans, and is still played in Italy nowadays.

Go
This is the world's oldest known game. It is still played in China.

Connect 4
This is a game for 2 players. Each player has to drop in the coloured discs and try to make a line of 4 in any direction and, at the same time, try to block their opponent.

Yote
Yote is a game which is played in Africa. You can get expensive sets to play with, or it can be played with pebbles and holes in the ground.

Bartholomew's Fair
Bartholomew's Fair was held each year, in London, in the Middle Ages. Hundreds of people would gather and play games, and watch cock fighting and wrestling.
Source: John Morley, *Memoirs of Bartholomew Fair,* 1874

There are other 'getting around' games. In Blind one's bluff, one player is blindfolded and has to try and catch any other player. Computer games come in many varieties and include fantasy games, arcade games and games of skill and stimulation. They often involve moving around the screen in a certain way.

Heinemann Educational *Technology Investigations*

What makes a good toy?

Read this article by Dr Dorothy Einon to help you answer the questions.

What makes a good toy?

**CHILD
EDUCATION
PRE-SCHOOL EXTRA**

**This was the question we put to Dr Dorothy Einon, lecturer in
psychology at University College, London**

A good toy helps a child to develop, to explore her capabilities and those of the world around her, and to expand her imagination. But first of all a toy must be fun to play with.

A toy attracts a child if it holds her attention and encourages interaction. The child has to be able to make something happen and to receive feedback from the toy. It also needs to capture her imagination.

The next consideration is the child's level of development. Choose toys which provide the child with what she needs to know at her stage of development.

Various skills develop throughout the nought to five period, through play with water, sand, building toys, etc. These encourage the child to experiment, developing knowledge of the properties of materials, memory and various strategies, such as sorting and matching. Books, paints and crayons are also important from the age of about one. Ideally a good toy should be able to develop more than one skill.

By five, children should be given a choice in what toys you buy for them, as they will often be guided by what their friends have, and will want to collect sets.

**3
FEATURE**

Giving children toys which are too 'old' for them does not help them to progress faster, explains Dr Einon. They will only become bored with the toy and it will remain unused.

Her third priority is that a good toy should be safe and durable. If in doubt, refer to the 1975 Toy Safety Regulations.

Source: *Child Education, Pre-School Extra*

Questions

1 What three points does Dr Einon think are important about a good toy?
2 At different ages, what kinds of toys do children play with?
3 Find different ways of getting information about toy safety. You could write to toy companies, read articles and books and look at the British and European Standards.

Toy performance indicator

This chart shows the top 10 toys bought in Britain during four months in 1990.

Product	Company	March	April	May	June
The Real Ghostbusters	Tonka	1	1	1	1
Matchbox Cars & Accessories	Matchbox	2	2	2	2
Sylvanian Family	Tomy	4	3	3	3
Tomytime Pre-School	Tomy	6	6	6	4
Barbie	Mattel	8	8	8	5
Legoland Town	Lego	3	4	4	6
Fisher Price Pre-School Ranges	Fisher Price	9	11	9	7
Micro Machines	Rainbow	5	5	7	8
Duplo	Lego	7	9	5	9
Sindy	Hasbro	17	13	15	10

Source: *Toy Trader*, September 1990

Discuss and record

In a group, discuss the kinds of toys which make up this top 10 list. Why do you think they are so popular?

How does this choice of toys compare with those played with by:

◆ children you know   ◆ yourselves?

Why do you think children make different choices of toy? Record your findings.

Heinemann Educational **Technology Investigations**

Statements of attainment
Te 1/3a, 4b, c, 7d; **Te 2**/3c, 4a; **Te 4**/4c

Bags

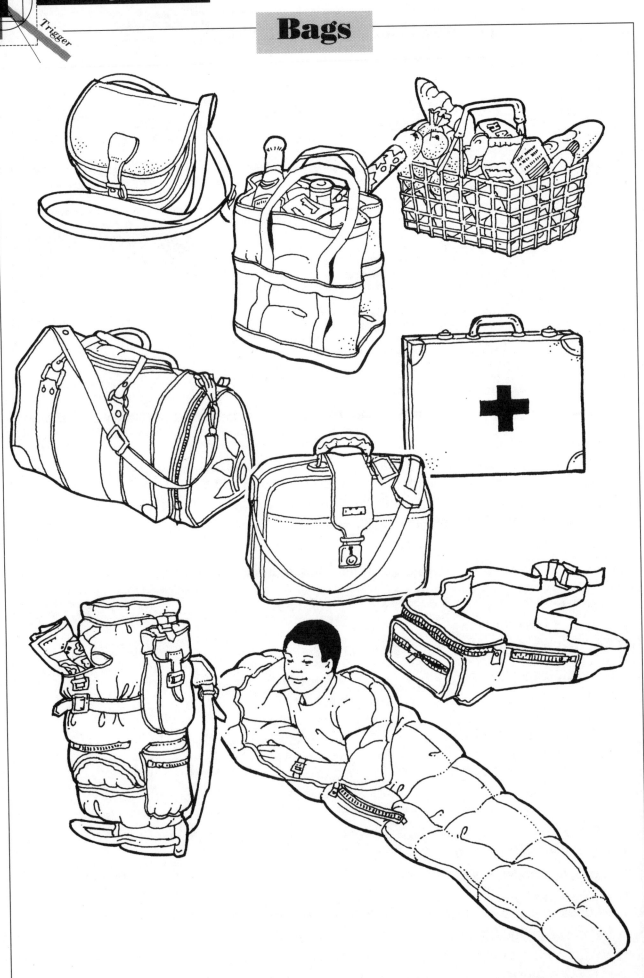

Heinemann Educational *Technology Investigations*

Designing a bag

For thousands of years, bags have been used for getting things around.
But what is a bag?
One dictionary says a bag is a receptacle of flexible material with an opening at the top.
Do you agree with this statement? Give your reasons.

Discuss and record

Bags have many uses.
Identify a need for carrying something around.
See how bags are used in your school environment.
Use Triggersheet 134 to give you ideas.
Make some quick sketches of some designs. Ask other people what they think about your ideas.
Could your designs have other uses?

Plan and make

Think about making your bag.
What materials could you choose?
Can you sew the bag together? Do you need to learn new skills?
How will the bag close?
Do you need to make a pattern?
Will you make a **prototype** in cheap fabric?
How much will it cost to make?
How will you test your design to see if it works?
Will you decorate your bag?
Record your ideas, using Sheet 136.

Evaluate

Compare your bag with others.
Are you pleased with the result?
Could you improve your design?
Could you make your bag?

The bum bag

Did you know?

The bum bag has been around for over 60 years. It was used by skiers and advertised as a small handy bag with a zip, fastened on a belt. Yet it was not until 1990 that the bum bag as a fashion accessory really took off.
Bum bags are useful for people of all ages. You can carry bits and pieces such as money, tissues, combs and sweets without weighing down your pockets.
The craze may be due to our greater awareness of security. People feel happier if their valuables are zipped to their middles rather than hanging in a bag over their shoulder.
Today bum bags are made in many colours and materials. Fabrics are decorated with logos, transfer pictures, sequins and glitter.
Design your own bum bag – it's the bottom line!

Heinemann Educational *Technology Investigations*

Statements of attainment

Te 1/3a, 4b, 7d; **Te 2**/3c, d, e, 5a, c, e, 6c, 7b, c; **Te 3**/3b, c, 4c; **Te 4**/4a, d, 5c

Bag design planning sheet

Designing a bag

Sketches to show ideas

Samples of fabrics which could be used

Bag design

Ideas for decoration

Pattern plans

Statements of attainment
Te 3/3a, 4c

Moving pictures

In the 18th century, scientists investigated many different ways to make pictures move. Some ideas were quite simple. Dr Paris invented a spinning disc with a picture on either side – for example, a bird and a cage. When the disc was spun the bird appeared in the cage – two pictures became one.

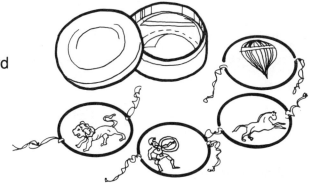

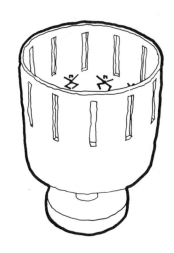

Another popular way to make moving images was to use a **zoetrope**. Strips of paper with drawings of horses or acrobats were fitted inside a spinning drum. When the drum was spun and anyone looked through the slots the image moved and the viewer saw horses jump and acrobats tumble.

You can make drawings look as if they are moving by flicking through a series of pictures. These pictures show the order in which something moves. For example, you can show someone kicking a football in the air.

The **mutoscope** applies this idea to photographs. You look through a viewfinder and turn a handle to see a series of moving images. These machines were later known as 'What the Butler Saw' and could be found at fairgrounds and in seaside arcades.

Making a zoetrope 1

Design and make
Design and make a zoetrope.

Equipment

- ◆ scissors
- ◆ a mechanism to make your drum spin

Materials

- ◆ card
- ◆ paper
- ◆ pens
- ◆ sellotape
- ◆ glue

Making the drum
You can follow this method or invent your own.

Method

- ◆ Cut out a strip of card 10 cm by 60 cm.
- ◆ Cut out small slots at even intervals near the top of the length of the strip. These are for looking through.
- ◆ Stick the ends of the card together to make a cylinder shape.
- ◆ Cut out a circular base which will fit on to the bottom of your cylinder to make the drum.

slots

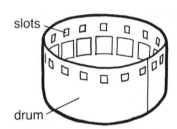
slots

drum

Ways of making the drum spin
Here are some ideas to make the drum spin. Try to think of others.

- ◆ Fix your drum on to an old record player – make sure it works first!
- ◆ Use a large drawing pin pushed through the base of the drum and into a cork.
- ◆ Tape a stick or a pencil to the base of the drum.
- ◆ The base of a rotary salad drier, turned upside-down, will spin. Fix the drum on top.

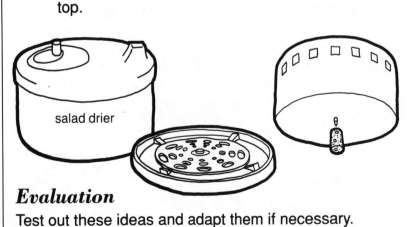
salad drier

Evaluation
Test out these ideas and adapt them if necessary.

Heinemann Educational *Technology Investigations*

Statements of attainment
Te 2/3b, c, 5d; **Te 3**/3b, c, 4c; **Te 4**/6b

Making a zoetrope 2

Drawing your moving images

Think of a theme for your pictures. It could be moving faces, circus tricks, people walking.

◆ Draw or use a computer program to design a series of pictures which show someone or something moving.

◆ Stick the pictures to a strip of paper which fits inside the drum.

◆ Test your zoetrope on your moving base. Ask other people what they think.

You may find that you need to adapt and improve your pictures at this stage, but keep the strips to show your progress.

Evaluation

Show your zoetrope to other class members. Explain to them how it was made and how you adapted ideas as you worked.

Write a report or make a tape recording to explain how you designed and made your zoetrope. Think about what problems you faced and how you overcame them. Include examples of your picture strips to show your progress.

Do you think today's children would enjoy playing with a zoetrope?

Give your reasons.

Heinemann Educational *Technology Investigations*

Statements of attainment
Te 2/3c, e, 5a; **Te 3**/3c, 4c; **Te 4**/3a, b, 4a

Whacky ways of getting around

There are lots of different ways of getting around.
Here are three whacky inventions that were designed and made in the past.

Jumping shoes

These were designed in 1922 to help
children to run and jump further when
playing. They could be worn over
ordinary shoes, and a buckle held
them in place. The three steel legs on
either side were very strong and springy. Each leg had a rubber pad on the bottom to
soften landings and help the wearer avoid injuries.

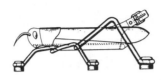
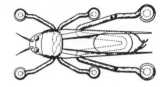

Pram

This elaborate pram was designed in the shape of a
shoe, complete with laces and an umbrella to keep rain
or sun off the baby's head. The inventor hoped that
wealthy parents might prefer this fun model to the other
designs.

Steam carriage

This steam carriage was designed to carry
small packages through crowded streets. The
chest of the 'iron man' contained a steam
engine which powered the two metal legs.
Smoke and excess steam escaped through
the head and top hat. The driver sat in the
cart and controlled the size of the steps.
Since the steam engine was very small the
carriage needed to stop often to refuel, so it
could only be used over short distances.

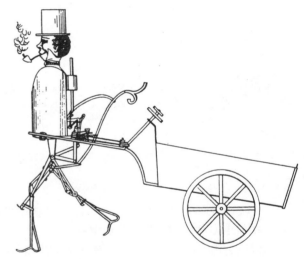

Evaluation

Carry out this evaluation in groups.
What do you think about these designs?

- ◆ Are they useful?
- ◆ Do they meet a need?
- ◆ Would they work?
- ◆ Do you think they were successful?

Write a short report evaluating each design.

Design and make

Design your own whacky invention for getting around.

Ideas!

- ◆ You could use a computer program to help you design your invention.
- ◆ Think about how your invention will be operated.
- ◆ What purpose will it have?

Heinemann Educational *Technology Investigations*

Statements of attainment
Te 1/4f, 5b; **Te 2**/3c, 4d; **Te 4**/4c, d, 5b

Eating on the go

In recent years more and more people in Britain are 'eating on the go' – nibbling snacks and eating takeaway meals as they move around.
Food companies are designing new products to meet this need.
How do companies identify the need for a new food?

Discuss and record

Look at the packet design for Apple Crackles.
Work in a group and discuss:

◆ when people would eat this food

◆ what age group you think it is aimed at (the **target group**)

◆ what sort of lifestyle you think they lead.

Record your findings
Your notes show what is known as the **product profile** for this food.

Evaluation

Do you think there is a need for this product? Explain your answers.
How does this product compare with other similar foods for sale?
Do you think it will be successful and sell well?
What improvements, if any, would you suggest?

Further work

Make a collection of other new food products.
Carry out an evaluation of them and discuss whether they will be successful, and why.

Statements of attainment

Te 1/3a, 4b, 5b; **Te 2**/3c, 4a; **Te 4**/4c, d, 6d

Takeaway food

Top of the takeaways

By JACK DAVIS, Consumer Affairs Correspondent

BRITONS eat more fast food than any other nation in Europe, a survey reveals.

We spent £3.28 billion last year — £25 a head—on hamburgers, pizzas, fish and chips and other takeaways.

And although Americans still top the takeaway table, with £138 a head in 1989, the switch from restaurant meals to 'snacking' means sales are growing faster on this side of the Atlantic. The Italians, with the fastest growing market, and West Germans are also big on fast food, say researchers, Euro-monitor. In the UK, fast food sales — up 13 per cent last year — are expected to increase by around 11 per cent a year over the next four years.

We still like burgers best. They account for just over half of takeaway sales. But pizzas are the success story of recent years, now claiming 36 per cent of the market. 'This growth has been helped by the expansion of home delivery services and by the wide consumer appeal of pizza as a more sophisticated meal than burgers,' says the report. The burger chains are fighting back, by offering a wider range of takeaways including breakfasts, fish and chicken meals, vegetarian burgers and salads.

The report says sandwich bar sales in the UK were worth £660million last year — up nearly 14 per cent since 1987 — and are now worth £30million less than takeaways from chip shops, which are declining.

Although pasta-loving Italy still eats less fast food than any other Europeans, it had a 22 per cent increase in sales last year. Hamburgers still dominate in Germany, with McDonald's accounting for 41 per cent of the £800 million takeaway market.

In France the fast food chains face fierce competition from restaurants, cafes and bistros, but are expected to flourish this decade. Hamburgers are the favourite fast food of the French, followed by croissants, brioches, pastries, sandwiches and pizzas. Euromonitor predicts that changes in Eastern Europe may have set the scene for a fast food revolution—started by the opening of a McDonald's in Moscow.

Source: *Daily Mail*, 30 July 1990

Read the newspaper article above.

Answer the following questions.
1   How much does each person in Britain spend a year on fast food?
2   What is the percentage increase in sales of fast food in Britain in 1989?
3   What is the most popular takeaway food in Britain?
4   Why are sales of fast food increasing in Britain?
5   In what way are other countries in Europe changing their eating habits?

Further work

1   Design a questionnaire to find out the range of takeaway food eaten by your friends. You could put your findings into a computer database.
2   Compare your questionnaire results with the survey shown in the article. What do they both show?
3   What types of takeaway food do you think we will be eating in the year 2000? Use the answers from your questionnaire and the newspaper article to help you with this work.

Keep a record of your ideas. These could be:
 ◆ notes
 ◆ drawings
 ◆ both.

Heinemann Educational *Technology Investigations*

Statements of attainment

Te 1/3a, 4b, 5b, 6a, 7b; **Te 2**/3c, 4a, d, 5c; **Te 4**/4d

Designing a new fast food 1

Imagine that your group works for a food company that wants to design a range of new fast foods that can be eaten on the move. Choose one of the **product briefs** shown below.

BRIEF 1

Design a range of breakfast foods which are either ready to eat or quickly prepared – a 'Ready breakfast kit'.

BRIEF 2

The company wants to produce a range of 'Healthy snacks' for teenagers. Think up some ideas.

BRIEF 3

Design a range of 'One pack meals' which are quick to prepare or ready to eat.

All these new foods must meet **3 criteria**. They must be:

◆ easy to eat

◆ reasonably healthy

◆ 'green' – environmentally friendly.

Getting ideas

In your team **brainstorm** ideas for the product brief which you have chosen. This is known as **concept generation**. When you brainstorm, remember:

◆ all ideas, however whacky, should be written down

◆ everyone has a point of view

◆ a spider diagram can help to organize your brainstorming.

self heating cans of food?

breakfast kit.

porridge in a pot

A spider diagram often helps

Choosing the best idea

Working as a team you now need to sort through your brainstorming ideas. Decide which ones *best* meet the product brief. Choose 3 to develop further. This method of sorting out ideas is used by industry to reject designs and products which may be unsuitable because they:

◆ cost too much

◆ would not sell well

◆ cannot be made easily.

This is known as **concept screening**.

Heinemann Educational *Technology* Investigations

Statements of attainment

Te 1/3a, 4b, c, 7c; **Te 2**/3a, c, e, 4a, d, 5a; **Te 4**/4d

Designing a new fast food 2

Product screening

Your team must now come up with *one* idea for the food range. Reject any ideas which do not meet the 3 criteria:

◆ easy to eat   ◆ healthy   ◆ 'green image'.

Check the 3 criteria

Think about these factors.

◆ Are there other similar foods on the market?
◆ Do you know how to make the product?
◆ If not, can you find out?
◆ Can it be sold throughout the year?

What other factors has your group taken into account?
Explain how and why you have come to your final choice.

Marketing plan

At this stage a food company would think about how to market its new product.
There are four main factors to consider:

◆ how it will be packaged
◆ how it will be priced
◆ where in the store it will be sold
◆ how it will be promoted.

In your team decide on a **marketing plan** for your food range.

Packaging

Keep a record of your planning as you go along.

◆ How will you protect your food and keep it safe to eat?
◆ Think about the 'green' image.
◆ Will you pack in large or small numbers?
◆ What details will you provide on the pack?
◆ Have you considered the cost?

Heinemann Educational **Technology Investigations**

Designing a new fast food 3

Record

Explain how and why you have made decisions about your product design.

Name and logo

What name will you give your new food?
Work on a design for the company logo.
Use Activity sheets 146 and 149 to help.

Price

What price range will you
choose? Will it be:

- ◆ low to attract interest
- ◆ mid point
- ◆ high for quality?

Where will the food be sold in the store?

- ◆ fresh food section
- ◆ frozen compartments
- ◆ on grocery shelves
- ◆ in chill cabinets
- ◆ aisle or aisle end?

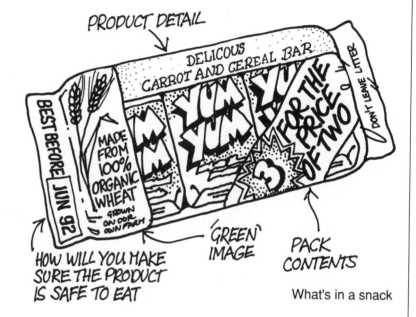

PRODUCT DETAIL

DELICOUS CARROT AND CEREAL BAR

BEST BEFORE JUN 92

MADE FROM 100% ORGANIC WHEAT GROWN ON OUR OWN FARM

YUM YUM YUM

3 FOR THE PRICE OF TWO

DON'T LEAVE LITTER

HOW WILL YOU MAKE SURE THE PRODUCT IS SAFE TO EAT

'GREEN' IMAGE

PACK CONTENTS

What's in a snack

Promotion

How will you let people know about your new range of foods?

- ◆ advertise in newspapers and magazines
- ◆ special offers
- ◆ shop demonstrations and leaflets
- ◆ TV campaign

Evaluate

Talk to your teacher and classmates about all that you have done.
Think about:

- ◆ how you arrived at your final decisions
- ◆ if you have achieved your design brief
- ◆ how you have worked together as a team
- ◆ ways in which your ways of working and ideas could be improved.

Heinemann Educational *Technology Investigations*

Statements of attainment

Te 1/3a, 4e, 5b, 6a, c, 7c; **Te 2**/3a, b, c, e, 4a, d, 5a, c, 6a, b, c; **Te 3**/3b, 4b; **Te 4**/4a, b, 5b

Designing a name

Ah! Bisto!

Up until the last century cooks made gravy by thickening meat juices with flour and adding seasoning and water. This was a lengthy and not always satisfactory business. There was a need for food manufacturers to develop a product that would brown, season and thicken all in one go. Legend has it that Mrs McRobert and Mrs Patterson, whose husbands worked for the Cerebos food company, raised the gravy problem one night over dinner.

After much experimenting, the company's chemists came up with a dry powder which, when mixed with water and blended with the juices from the roasting tin, produced a thick, well-seasoned, rich brown gravy.

The Cerebos company now needed a name for their product. By playing with various combinations of the initials of the selected slogan – 'Browns, Seasons, Thickens — In One' – they came up with the name that has been part of the English language now for 75 years: Bisto.

Further work

1   Other products have specially designed names. Carry out some research to find out the history behind some of these names: Bird's custard, Biro, Coca Cola, Heinz, Kelloggs, Lego, Plasticine, Yale Locks.
    You could look in books and write to the companies.

2   Invent your own name for a product of your choice. Write a short story to explain how the name came about.

Heinemann Educational Technology Investigations

----- *Statements of attainment* -----
Te 1/3a, 4b, f, 5a, 7d; **Te 2**/3c

Packaging designs

Cadbury's dairy milk chocolate

Packaging protects the product inside. However, packaging design plays a less obvious role.

In the 19th century sweets, like other goods, were mostly *not* prepackaged. The shopkeeper would weigh out and pack goods for customers. Prepackaging changed all this – the packaging now became the *salesperson* for the product and shops became **self-service**.

Over the years, as the number of products in competition with each other has increased so, too, has the importance of packaging design. Today, strong colours and bold, simple graphics shout at you from the supermarket shelves, trying to attract your attention. Manufacturers change packaging designs to update them. These changes must be slight, otherwise customers might think that the product is different. So, although the wrappers for Cadbury's chocolate have undergone a series of changes since they were introduced in the last century, the **colours** – purple for milk chocolate and red for plain – have not changed.

Discuss

Look at the pictures of the packaging designs for Kellogg's Corn Flakes.
How have they changed over the years?
What has remained the same?
Why do you think changes have been made?

Research

Carry out some research into how packaging has changed over the years.

Heinemann Educational *Technology Investigations*

Statements of attainment
Te 1/3a, 4f, 5b; **Te 2**/3c; **Te 4**/4c, d

Naming products

No holds barred in making a name stick

You can no longer buy a Marathon chocolate bar in the UK. Britain's fourth favourite snack bar has been renamed **Snickers**. The manufacturer, Mars, insist that it is the same product with the same amount of chocolate, nuts and goo. So why did they change the name?

The answer lies with Mars's global branding strategy – the bar is known as Snickers in every market except the UK. Mars want their products to be known by the same name across Europe. What were once Treets are now M&Ms, and Munchies cat food has become Brekkies.

Other companies are following Mars's example and using the same name for their products across Europe. Unilever's washing powder Radion is the same in most European markets. Global branding can save companies money. Standardization results in production costs being cut and advertising costs can also be reduced by using the same images with different words.

Source: adapted from an article by Tim Hindle, *Daily Telegraph*, July 23 1990

Questions

Use the article to help you answer the following questions.

1   Which chocolate bar has been given a new name? Why was the decision made?

2   What is meant by 'global branding'? How does global branding save companies money?

Research

Look around your home or visit the shops. Find 10 products which are made in other countries yet have familiar brand names.

Heinemann Educational **Technology Investigations**

Statements of attainment
Te 1/3a, 4b, 5b; **Te 4**/4c, d

Getting around logos

Logos may be symbols and/or words used to identify companies, products and places. This is the logo for the Trocadero shopping centre in Piccadilly Circus, London. It symbolizes what the Trocadero is all about – 'Fun, food and fashion'.

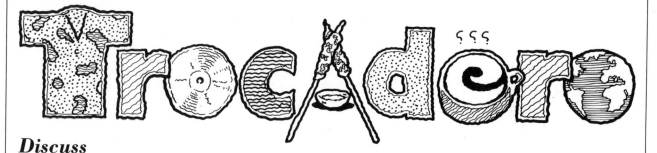

Discuss

Below are the logos for some of the top products sold around the world. Make a list of those you recognize.

Research

Make a collection of logos which identify different products, places and companies.

Evaluate

Discuss which ones you think work best and why.

Design a logo

Work in a small team. Decide who will do what. You will need to:

◆ record ideas   ◆ make drawings   ◆ do a presentation to the class.

Think up a logo for the product, place or company of your choice. You have half an hour to design the logo. Keep a record of all the stages you go through. Present your logo to the rest of the class and ask them for their views. Adapt your design if necessary. Think about these ideas:

1   How does your logo identify the product?
2   What market is it aimed at?
3   Where will your logo be seen . . . shops, bags, packets?
4   How does it compare to other logos with the same theme?
5   What makes your logo special to the product, place or company it is advertising?

─── *Statements of attainment* ───
Te 1/3a, 5b, 7c; **Te 2**/3a, c, e, 4a, d, 5a, 6a, b, 7b, c; **Te 3**/4b, e, 6a; **Te 4**/3a, 4c, d, 5a

Design an image board

When designers want to brainstorm ideas to help them design things like logos, advertisements and company symbols they sometimes prepare an **image board**.
An image board can be a collection of pictures and sketches to trigger design ideas. The pictures are chosen to meet the needs of the design brief. The image board below was designed for this brief.

Design brief
Design a logo or symbols which can be used to market and package our product. It must be simple, elegant and imaginative and also show how we care for people all around the world.

Image board

Design ideas

◆ Use the image board shown above and come up with 10 ideas for the logo or symbol to meet the design brief. Present your ideas to others and ask for their views.

◆ Create your own image board for a design brief of your choice.

Heinemann Educational **Technology Investigations**

Getting around

Adapting a wheelchair 1

When Daphne Bessant started to use a wheelchair to get around, she soon found that the basic design did not meet her needs – so she made some changes. Being an ex-teacher, Daphne has a sense of fun, so not all the extras are essential!

Before setting off on a trip Daphne checks the battery, which is carried under the wheelchair, to see if it needs recharging. Daphne's wheelchair is capable of travelling 24 km at just over 6 km per hour – enough for a 3 hour journey.

Since Daphne has trouble breathing, she carries an oxygen cylinder strapped to the front of the wheelchair, which contains 20 minutes supply of gas. For an emergency, she keeps a 'Help' flag in a side pocket.

Daphne explains why she has the long pole carrying three coloured flags. 'My home is over a hump back bridge and cars can see the flags as I approach and slow down instead of running me over! The top flag says "Stop what you are doing and watch!", but I'm not sure all motorists understand the meaning.'

'Joggling' in a wheelchair up curbs and along bumpy roads has its hazards. 'You can easily tip out of the chair, so I have made a high back with two broom handles and safety straps to hold me in. I have padded the armrests and replaced the rigid footrest with a swing structure so I can put my feet down easily. The tow rope at the back is strong enough to pull my friend's wheelchair so we can go out together.'

Daphne travels in all weathers and has packed the wheelchair with a rain cape, hat and warm blanket. If it's hot, she can switch on the fan. There are several bags to carry shopping and hold kit such as lipstick, loo rolls and wet wipes.

Just like a car, the wheelchair has front and rear lights, a wing mirror and two hooters. One last adaptation: 'Friends lean on my wheelchair for a chat and hit the "On" switch and send me hurtling off down the road, so I've invented a plastic cover to stop them starting up the wheelchair accidentally!'

Design ideas

- ◆ How could you adapt a wheelchair to meet special needs? Have a look at wheelchair designs and sketch some ideas.
- ◆ Talk to someone who uses a wheelchair. Find out what problems they face when trying to get around. What are their needs?
- ◆ Try out a wheelchair and record the problems you find with the design. Suggest adaptations.
- ◆ Look at some old pictures of wheelchairs. How have designs changed for modern use?

Questions

Choose the 'top 3' of Daphne's changes to her wheelchair.
Why do you think these are the cleverest?
Give your reasons.

Statements of attainment

Te 1/3a, b, 4b, c, f, 5a, b, 6c, 7c, d; **Te 2**/3c, e, 4a, 5c, 7b; **Te 3**/6e; **Te 4**/4c, d

Heinemann Educational *Technology Investigations*

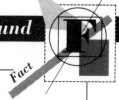
Adapting a wheelchair to meet people's needs

Profiles

Annie

Annie is 25, and works in London as a research scientist. She has her own car and needs her wheelchair to get around the laboratory and busy streets.

Annie has an active social life and often goes to the theatre and out for a meal.

Darren

Darren is a policeman who was injured whilst on duty and is now confined to a wheelchair.

He has a wife and two young children and likes to take them out for day trips at weekends. The whole family find the wheelchair useful to carry things around.

Darren takes part in the paraplegic games and visits the gym twice a week to keep fit.

Jay

Jay is 11 and has just started comprehensive school. He needs to carry all his school things around with him, as well as a pullover and anorak in case it gets cold.

Jay goes to the local basketball club and likes to visit McDonalds for a snack in the evening.

Doris

Doris is 70 and has severe arthritis. She finds it difficult to use her hands to push or hold things.

Doris lives on her own in a small ground floor flat and likes to do her own washing and cooking. Doris often goes out and takes her small dog to the park.

Adapting a wheelchair 2

Discuss and record

Look at Factsheet 153. The four people profiled each get around in a wheelchair.
Look at the basic model drawn here. How could this wheelchair be adapted to meet each of their needs? Use Activity sheet 152, Factsheet 153 and Triggersheet 151 for ideas.
Working in groups, choose one person to design for. Discuss what extras you might include on a wheelchair for that person.
Record and sketch your ideas.
Ask others to comment on your work.

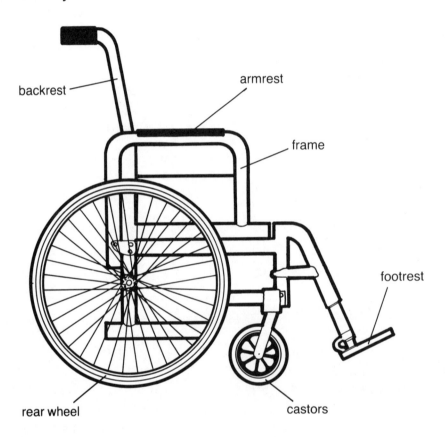

backrest · armrest · frame · footrest · rear wheel · castors

Design and make

Could you adapt a **real** wheelchair?
If you can borrow a wheelchair, then why not try out your ideas?
Decide who you are adapting the wheelchair for.
You need not use expensive materials – broom handles, bags, string and other household objects will do.

Evaluation

Test and evaluate your design to see if it meets the original needs.
You could contact manufacturers and find out what extras they sell for wheelchairs.
Compare their catalogues with your ideas.

Heinemann Educational *Technology Investigations*

Statements of attainment
Te 1/3a, 4c, 5b, 7d; **Te 2**/3c, d, 4a; **Te 3**/3b, 4b, e; **Te 4**/5a

Design a wheelchair for yourself

Write a **design specification** for your own wheelchair.

> **What is a design specification?**
>
> A design specification is a way of describing special things which are needed for that design. So, a wheelchair might need to be:
> - speedy
> - lightweight
> - brightly coloured.

To think up a design specification for your own wheelchair, you must identify what you do each day and how the wheelchair can help you get around.

Research

How do you spend your day?

Keep a diary over 1–2 days. Write down the different activities you take part in each day and note when there might be problems if you were using a wheelchair.

Think about:
- how often you get in and out of cars
- busy streets, curbs, steps and stairs
- the sports you play
- what you do for fun, e.g. shopping, walks in the country, going to the cinema . . . any other activities.

Wheelchair designs

Your research can help you sort out your needs. You could draw up a chart to help organize your ideas.

Need	Design features to meet these needs
to get in and out of cars easily	the wheelchair must be lightweight

What 'extras' do you need?
- bags
- hooter
- tennis racket holder . . .

Design specification

To help you write your design specification you may need expert help.

You could ask:
- other wheelchair users to give you ideas
- wheelchair manufacturers to send you their brochures
- magazines and other sources of information such as NERIS.

Record your ideas

These can all help:
- notes
- sketches
- scale drawings
- photos.

Now write your design specification for your own wheelchair.

Ask other people for their opinion.

Does the design meet all your needs?

Heinemann Educational *Technology Investigations*

Statements of attainment

Te 1/3a, b, 4b, c, e, 5b, 7d; **Te 2**/3a, b, c, 4a, d, 5a, 6a, b; **Te 4**/3a, 4d

Wheelchair specifications

This is the design specification for a Swede Elite wheelchair. A design specification can describe the special features, materials and measurements which may be chosen for the design.

SWEDE ELITE DESIGN SPECIFICATION
Swede Elite is a lightweight wheelchair with an all welded frame. The frame weighs under 5 kg. It is easy to handle, stable, stylish and small when folded.
It offers a range of sizes and adjustments to match each person's needs.

Standard features

24" rear wheels, quick release. High pressure tubeless tyres.
Titanium handrims, oval section for maximum grip.
One-piece titanium footrest.
High-mounted aluminium brakes.
Calf support, nylon with velcro.
5" castor assembly.
High-precision sealed bearings.
3-degree camber on rear axle.
Polyester upholstery, washable at 40deg C.
Tyre pump, instruction manual and tools.

Design features

Seat – adjustable for height and angle.
Castor assembly – adjustable for angle.
Long or short seat frame.
Seat upholstery adjustable for depth.
Backrest angles: +3, 0, −5, −10 degrees.
Backrest height adjustable 30–40 cm (12–16").
Adjustable centre of gravity.
Tension adjustments on seat and backrest upholstery for optimum comfort and posture control.

Materials

titanium	for frame, backrest and footrest
aluminium	castors and axle
steel	front fork
polyester lacquer	frame
black polyester	upholstery
Colour range:	green, blue, lilac, red, black

Questions

Use the Swede Elite design specification to help answer the following questions. You may need to find more information from wheelchair manufacturers or books to help.
1 What two features do you think are important in this design?
2 **Design features** Why do you think it is a good idea that the seat and backrest can be adjusted?
   Standard features Name two standard features which you think are important. Give your reasons.
3 Name three materials used to make this wheelchair.
   Choose one material and explain why it has been chosen for this design.
4 What colour would you choose for a wheelchair frame? Why?

Statements of attainment
Te 4/4c, 6c

Heinemann Educational *Technology Investigations*

Wheelchair sports

In 1992, nearly 4000 athletes will enter the **International Paralympics** in Barcelona, Spain. Many of those athletes need specially adapted wheelchairs for their different sports.

Rules for able-bodied people are changed to take account of the wheelchairs.

Design adaptations for sports wheelchairs

Wheelchairs for sports are lightweight and can spin around easily. The wheels are positioned at an angle of 60° or 70° to make the wheelchair more stable and better balanced. Armrests can be moved and back pieces fold or slide out.

In **basketball**, the armrests are removed and the back of the chair is low so that players can swing and move quickly. Special caster wheels allow the chair to spin and move smoothly.

In wheelchair **tennis**, the ball may bounce twice to give the players more time.

Wheelchairs for **discus throwing** are strapped down and must be a certain height so that players do not have advantages over each other.

Players often prefer to have no brakes on these wheelchairs. They stop the wheels with their hands.

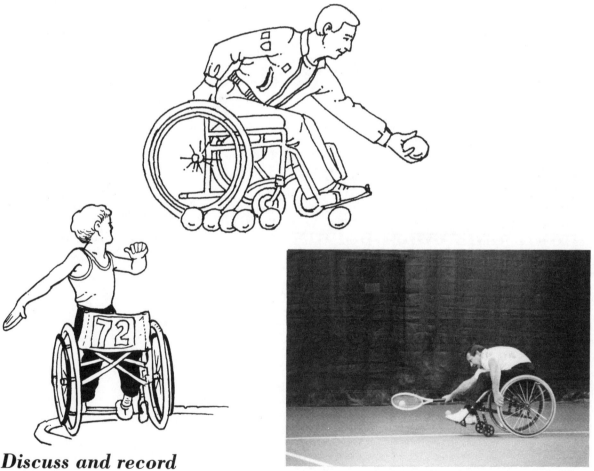

Discuss and record

Look at the different wheelchair sport activities in the pictures.

How have the wheelchairs been adapted to meet the needs of each sport?

Statements of attainment
Te 1/4c, 5b, 6c; **Te 2**/3c; **Te 4**/4c

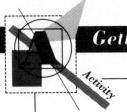

Historical evaluation of wheelchairs

Historical evaluation

Look at this advertisement from *The Graphic*, 4 March 1905. How has the design of wheelchairs changed to meet the needs of today?

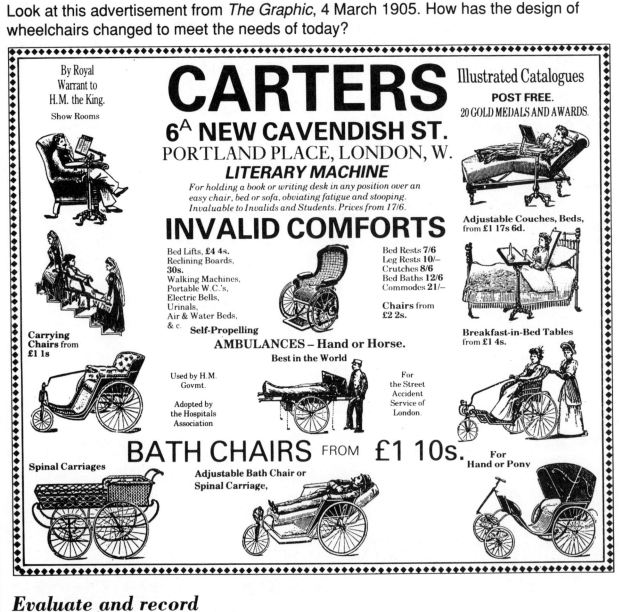

Evaluate and record

Choose one of these wheelchairs and evaluate its usefulness.

◆ Who would use it?

◆ Would it be comfortable?

◆ Can they move around easily in it?

Suggest some changes to its design to help it meed modern needs.

Heinemann Educational *Technology Investigations*

Statements of attainment
Te 1/4f, 5b, 6a, c; **Te 2**/3c; **Te 4**/4c

Index

Index